Start On Your Dreams

Start On Your Dreams

A Revolutionary Roadmap to Realizing
Dreams and Achieving Success

Jerry Coy

DEDICATION

To my beloved wife, Tina Coy, the cornerstone of my every endeavor and dream. To Angel, Alexis, Jordan, and Sadie - my guiding lights, the motivation that fuels my every step. Your love, laughter, and resilience inspire me daily, reminding me of life's immense possibilities.

And to all my students, whose ambition, challenges, and triumphs have ignited my passion to pen these pages. May this book reflect our shared journey, a testament to the power of dreams and the drive to make them a reality.

May you all find wisdom and inspiration in these words, and may they serve as a beacon of hope and determination for years to come.

TABLE OF CONTENTS

Jerry Coy

Preface

Charles Dickens started his great novel "*It Was the Best of Times; It Was the Worst of Times*." I'm stealing this line because of this unprecedented time. I'm referring to the most interesting year of the 21st century so far: 2020. I started this book project towards the end of 2020 because it was a very challenging year.

I am a teacher. At the time, I taught Anatomy & Physiology to high school students. We broke for spring break in the spring of 2020 and did not return to school until the 2021 academic year. You may remember schools closed campuses across the country. We got the email from the administrators two days before we were supposed to return to class on Monday. "We will now be finishing school online." Teachers had to learn to set up an online course in just a few days. My students did not sign up for an online course as I did not accept an online teaching position. About half of my students did not even have access to a computer, and some had no internet access at home. Although I believe I set up a pretty good online version of my class, some students started to get discouraged, and some gave up.

My students needed more motivation to continue. Especially since rumors were floating around that their grades would not be penalized due to the switch in venue, regardless of whether they did the work. At the time, I was teaching future nurses. I could not have them graduate nursing school without knowing the difference between a brain and a pancreas because I may one day be their patient. I had to do something. I started sharing motivational YouTube videos using the Remind app to text them. One of my favorite videos was "Before You Quit, Remember Why You Started." I even started making crude videos using my webcam. I created assignments for them to come up with their "why." Why did you enroll in my class? Why do you want to get into nursing? I taught them how to find their "*why*" and remember the feeling they felt when they started. I also embedded secret assignments into my lecture videos to ensure they were watching them. I gave them extra activities like writing down their dreams and goals. I was able to help all of them to complete my class.

The following fall semester, we did not teach classes online like most of the country. We were in the classroom only. I continued my motivational exercises and incorporated T.G.I.M. (Thank God It's Monday) every week. During that academic year, I developed the seven steps of success which are seven of chapters of unit 2 in this book. I refined these steps the following academic year and implemented them with my students.

Some years before I became a teacher, I worked for someone who mentored me for a few months. Terrance, who taught me about everything financial, introduced me to many things to improve myself. He taught me that the best investment I could make is in myself. He shared with me my first audiobook. He also shared his reading list with me. I live in a suburban community and have a very long commute. I've gotten tired of the noise on the radio, so I used my commute time to learn from audiobooks and podcasts. I got into audiobooks that helped me improve myself. I've listened to several motivational speakers, self-help gurus, financial "experts," "how-to" masters, coaches, and more. I've joined online tutorial sites and have taken several online courses. I also started to follow inspirational people on social media instead of useless distractions. In upcoming chapters, we will learn about the digital detox.

Since then, I've practiced motivational speaking with my students because I wanted them to succeed. They suggested I start a podcast or write a book. So, here's my book. You should also check out my podcast, "Start on Your Dreams." You can keep up with all my projects and find my social media at startonyourdreams.com.

Jerry Coy

Introduction

This book outlines the steps and principles to program your brain to achieve your goals. I teach about the brain in my class and have extensively studied neuroscience. We are going to use neuroscience to hack our brains. Many successful people in history were probably no more intelligent than the rest of us. The difference is that they had more motivation, focus, drive, and maybe even a little luck. There is a system in our brain that keeps us alert and focused. It's called the *reticular activating system* (RAS). It acts as a filter that keeps your thoughts on the topic and filters out irrelevant information. If your RAS is not programmed correctly, you may filter out what you need to succeed. Your brain will prioritize what is important by what you focus on. **Do not underestimate the power of your mind.**

I will give you an example of how this RAS works. This probably has happened to you. You're at the car dealership and notice a new model you're unfamiliar with. You've never seen one ever before. You then ask, "Is this a new model?" The salesman replies, "Not really." You test-drive it and do your due diligence. Maybe you can even buy it. It's the "new" Chevy Example. You are now driving home in your brand-new Chevy Example, and then you see another Chevy Example in front of you, then another, and another. You go to work the next day, and your coworker says she has one. Then your boss has one, too. Before you bought it, you've never seen a Chevy Example before now, they're everywhere. It is not because more people suddenly are driving the same car; it is because your RAS has been filtering out that information until you "activated" it.

Now imagine that your dreams and goals are manifesting instead of the Chevy Example manifesting everywhere. Several life coaches call it the "Law of Attraction." Which states like attracts like. Where attention goes, energy flows. I've heard it explained as a mysterious force that reads the energy you put out into the ether, and then the universe will manifest it for you. I prefer the neuroscience explanation for the rest of us who are not Jedi.

In this book, I compiled a series of exercises to program your brain so the RAS is working the way YOU want. Most of these principles are not new. Some are even centuries old. They have been used by highly successful people throughout history. I merely compiled these exercises into seven simple-to-understand steps. In the original draft of this book, I was going to put the seven steps in the first unit. Then, in unit two, I would get into other success principles as if they were an afterthought. The success principles I'm moving to the first unit are much more than just principles; they are crucial to preparing you so you're in the right mindset. In the right mindset, the seven steps in the second unit will be more effective. The second unit of this book will be the seven steps in the final chapters. Each chapter will be one of the seven steps. At the end of each chapter, there will be an exercise activity for you to complete. Sorry, I am a teacher and there will be homework. I recommend you do the exercises before moving on to the next chapter. It would be best to get a composition book and your favorite pen for these exercises. A spiral notebook will also work.

What this book is not all about.

This is not a book on how to get rich unless that is your goal. Success is not measured in dollar signs. I just Googled "define success," and it said, "the accomplishment of an aim or purpose." These success principles and exercises are about just that. It is up to you to figure out what that is. The first step will help you define what you want out of life. Success can be about money if you are about money. You can be successful in your professional life, but there is so much more. These steps can enhance your personal life, social life, health, and fitness and improve relationships. Organizations, companies, groups, and individuals can also use these seven steps.

Jerry Coy

Unit 1
Be in the Right Mind

The Mindset to Be Successful

Jerry Coy

Chapter 1
The Power of the Mind

"Your mind is a powerful thing.
When you fill it with positive thoughts,
your life will start to change."
~Unknown

Émile Coué was a French psychologist and apothecary during the turn of the twentieth century. He introduced the concept of *optimistic autosuggestion* as a method of psychotherapy for self-improvement. This method draws inspiration from early 20th-century ideas like Coué's "Every day, in every way, I'm getting better and better," aiming to reframe the subconscious into a more positive, constructive force. In a way, his techniques led to what is known as the placebo effect. Autosuggestion therapy uses self-induced suggestions to guide behavior, thoughts, and feelings. Self-hypnosis is a form of autosuggestion therapy. Autosuggestion can be intentional or unintentional. If you don't take control of your mind, unintentional autosuggestion may take control of your mind and your life. Autosuggestions have also been used in *psychoneuroimmunology* (PNI), using the power of the mind to control your health and resistance to disease. PNI and

11

autosuggestion are used to control pain and, in some cases, reverse disease. Autosuggestion is a cognitive process that enables control over one's cognitive and physiological states. (Myga et al. 2022)

There has been documented evidence that autosuggestion will either manifest or cure physiological disorders of the body. If you worry that you have a tumor in your body, your mind can manifest an actual tumor from the power of the mind. The power of the mind can also help shrink a tumor, especially if used in conjunction with diet, exercise, mindfulness, and medicine. Worry leads to stress, and stress has a physiological effect on the body's nervous system and hormones that can cause diabetes, cancer, cardiovascular disorders, hypertension, etc.

In sports psychology, the concept is also widely applied. Athletes often use positive affirmations and visualizations to prepare for competitions mentally. For example, Olympic swimmer Michael Phelps' long-term practice of visualizing successful races is well-documented, and he credits this mental preparation as a component of his athletic success.

Hans Seyle is known as the founder of the stress theory. He found the relationship between stress and disease. Selye's Syndrome, now known as General Adaptation Syndrome, is a chronic fight or flight where stress hormones and the sympathetic nervous system are aroused due to emotional or psychological stress. The acute form of fight or flight was first described by Walter Cannon in 1915. This demonstrates how the mind can also influence the body physiologically.

If you believe you will fail your final exam, it won't matter how much you study. You have already decided to fail. Your thoughts will set your destiny. Quantum consciousness, aka the quantum mind is a scientific hypothesis that proposes that classical mechanics cannot explain consciousness. Napoleon Hill believed that our brains are both receivers and transmitters of thought energy. Like the vibrations of energy through the ether of space, our thoughts can manifest into reality.

The idea that the mind can influence physical healing is a topic of interest across multiple disciplines, including psychology, medicine, and neuroscience. While it's important to stress that mind-based approaches are not a substitute for medical treatments, there are some documented studies and cases where psychological factors appear to have played a role in physical healing:

Placebo Effect: One of the most extensively studied phenomena in this area is the placebo effect. In numerous clinical trials, patients receiving a placebo (a sugar pill or saline injection, for example) often show symptom improvement simply because they believe they are receiving treatment.

Mindfulness-Based Stress Reduction (MBSR): Developed by Dr. Jon Kabat-Zinn, MBSR has been studied for its potential impact on various health outcomes, including chronic pain, stress, and mental well-being. Some studies have reported that these techniques can positively affect physiological markers like blood pressure and cortisol levels.

Cognitive Behavioral Therapy (CBT) for Pain Management: CBT effectively treats chronic pain conditions by changing pain perception. This doesn't "heal" the underlying disease but can improve quality of life and functionality.

Positive Psychological Interventions: Some studies have looked at how positive psychological interventions can influence post-surgical recovery times. While the effects are generally modest, evidence suggests that patients who engage in positive visualization or receive positive affirmation recover more quickly than those who do not.

Biofeedback: This technique teaches individuals how to influence physiological functions that are generally automatic, like heart rate. Some studies have shown that biofeedback can effectively treat headaches and high blood pressure.

Psychoneuroimmunology Studies: As mentioned earlier, the field of psychoneuroimmunology has produced research indicating that stress management and emotional well-being can positively affect immune function. However, this is not the same as "healing with the mind" in the sense that many people interpret it.

Guided Imagery: Some research suggests that guided imagery can help reduce postoperative pain and improve immune function. However, the evidence is still considered preliminary.

The power of the mind in manifesting your dreams cannot be overstated, and the 7-step process delineated in this book serves as a mental alchemy, transforming your thoughts into tangible realities. When you engage in this journey, you're not merely sketching out plans or gathering resources; you're rewiring your mental framework to align with your deepest desires. This is a conscious orchestration of cognitive abilities, wherein every thought, every decision, and every action becomes a deliberate step toward making your dreams come true. Once programmed through these steps, the mind becomes an invincible force geared toward realization and accomplishment.

As you navigate through each step—from defining what truly matters to you, setting precise objectives, and building an infallible action plan—you're not just making external moves. You are sculpting your mental landscape to become a fertile ground where dreams can take root and flourish. You're training your mind to be resilient in the face of adversity, focused amidst distractions, and adaptable when conditions are less than ideal. Your mental resilience and focus become the scaffolding that supports the manifestation of your dreams, turning once-elusive aspirations into achievable milestones.

By the time you've embraced and executed the 7-step process, your mind will be an engine of creation, fine-tuned and calibrated for success. You'll find that the boundaries between thought and reality begin to blur. Once figments of imagination, your dreams transform into concrete goals and tangible achievements. In the grand tapestry of life, your thoughts are the threads, and this process teaches you to weave them into a masterpiece of your own making. Mastering your mind becomes the ultimate tool in manifesting the life you've always dreamed of.

Jerry Coy

Start On Your Dreams

Chapter 2
Brief Overview of Basic Neuroscience

"Knowledge is power, but knowledge about yourself is self-empow-erment."
– Dr. Joe Dispenza

Spanish scientist Santiago Ramón y Cajal is known as the father of neuroscience. For this book you don't need to know this, but I'm a teacher, and I cannot help myself. Neuroscience is a primary course of study and even a specialty in medicine and psychology. One could study it for a lifetime and still not know all there is to know about neuroscience. I will go over it in this chapter, a very basic overview.

The brain and spinal cord make up the central nervous system. The peripheral nervous system goes out to the body. The brain has different levels of function. The higher part of the brain physically has higher functions, and the lower part has lower functions. The closest to the brain stem is the more basic of instinct and automated functions. The cerebral cortex is higher cognitive thought and behaviors. The prefrontal cortex, part of the cerebral cortex, is where decision-making and judgment happen. The prefrontal cortex is not fully developed in teenagers, which explains why teenagers don't always make the best decisions. There's a lot more to the brain that I cover in my class, but for this book, I won't bore you with it.

The brain also has structures that work together and function as systems. I want to discuss the limbic and reticular activating systems (RAS). These systems of the brain can control you and mislead you. I want you to know how these systems work so you can take charge of your basic programming. In other words, don't listen to your brain. Your brain has been programmed by thousands of years of instincts and behaviors. These primitive survival instincts protect you and will keep you alive, driving you beyond that.

The limbic system, the paleomammalian cortex, is responsible for behavior and emotional responses to stimuli. It is the source of primitive survival instincts. It is tied to the sense of smell so that we can smell predators and prey. The sense of smell will alert you to spoiled food or poisons. The sense of smell is also associated with sexual stimuli. A structure within the limbic system is the amygdala. The functions of the amygdala are known as "the four Fs": Feeding, Fighting, Fleeing, and Fornicating (the other F-word that means fornicating). Most students don't know the word fornicating, and I cannot say "fucking" in front of a public high school class. That will be the only time I use that word in this book. The purpose of the four Fs is basically to survive: not just for you, the individual, but for the human species. The amygdala makes you reproduce so humans can continue and pass on genes.

Jerry Coy

The amygdala is part of the lower brain functions, and if you listen to your amygdala, you will be doing nothing but raising babies or paying child support for the rest of your life. The lower brain functions need to be overridden by the higher brain functions. The male amygdala tends to be programmed to multiply. It is all about quantity. A more basic male brain wants to impregnate every woman in town. The basic female amygdala tends to be all about the quality of offspring. A more basic female brain wants strong and secure offspring, and they want to "nest." The more basic women are attracted to "muscles and money." The more evolved men and women want more than what the amygdala wants. A more evolved male realizes that if he impregnates every woman in town, he will be very unhappy paying child support and having 30 baby mammas. A more evolved woman knows that to be tied down with a basic muscle-head man would make a miserable existence. Today's evolved women desire more. Now that you know what your brain tells you, you can override those basic instincts and focus on what you want.

> *"Men and women need to appreciate their inherent differences and accept each other with respect."*
> *~ John Gray*

This is not intended to reinforce gender stereotypes. Instead, it offers an illustrative perspective on our brain's paleomammalian and reptilian aspects, harking back to a period when the human brain was in the earlier stages of its evolution. Yet, traces of these ancient structures persist within us today.

The amygdala and the limbic system are also responsible for your fear responses like fight or flight. Your fear of failure will keep you in your comfort zone. Nothing will crush your dreams and goals more than staying in your comfort zone. In this book, exercises and activities will help you override the limbic system and overcome your fear of trying.

The reticular activation system (RAS) keeps you alert and filters out information your higher brain doesn't need. While I am watching the television, my wife will be on the phone or talking to the children and dogs. My RAS alerts me to the dialog on the TV and filters out my wife. My wife will then start talking to me, but my RAS is still filtering her out in favor of the dialog on my show. I keep telling her she needs to call out my name if she wants my attention. How often has someone tried to communicate with you, but you don't hear them until they call out your name or get your attention? Your RAS will also filter out what it thinks is unimportant to you. If you are not thinking of opportunities, you may miss them. Unfortunately, your RAS doesn't know what is important to you and can filter out things you want. The seven steps in this book will help you program your brain to focus your RAS on your dreams and goals.

Where attention goes, energy flows. Remember the example of the RAS I gave in the introduction? You will never notice the Chevy Example until it is on your mind, and then you see them everywhere. You are now paying attention to it, and your brain is alerted. Only then will we stop filtering it out. You are now telling your brain what to filter and what to keep. So, we will stop listening to our amygdala and tell the RAS what to pay attention to.

One of the primary roles of the RAS is to prioritize information that matches our current beliefs, focus, or needs. Hence, "programming" the RAS can help steer our attention towards goals or ideas, making them easier to achieve or internalize. Here are some exercises to aid in programming the RAS:

1. Positive Affirmations: Our brain tends to focus on things that affirm our self-beliefs, whether positive or negative. Introducing daily positive affirmations into our routine can guide our RAS to prioritize positive information that aligns with these affirmations. Over time, the constant repetition ingrains these beliefs in our system. For instance, rather than telling yourself, "I'm not good at this," switch it to "I'm getting better every day." This not only uplifts your spirits but also programs your RAS to recognize opportunities for improvement.

2. Visual Imagery: This goes beyond just visual cues. Take a few moments each day to vividly imagine achieving your goals. If it's a new job, visualize yourself in that role, performing tasks, attending meetings, and receiving accolades. The key is to make the visualization as detailed and rich as possible. By doing this, your RAS becomes attuned to any information or opportunity that can make that visualization a reality.

3. Daily Journaling: Spend a few minutes each morning or evening writing about your goals, your steps toward them, and your achievements. This practice affirms your progress and programs your RAS to notice opportunities and resources that align with your objectives.

4. Gratitude Practice: List three things you're grateful for daily. It seems simple, but gratitude can shift your RAS's focus from what's lacking or negative in your life to the abundance and positivity that exists. Over time, you'll notice more things to be grateful for, and this positive focus can ripple into other areas of your life.

5. Environment Design: Surround yourself with images, quotes, books, and people who align with your goals and values. Your RAS will pick up on these consistent cues in your environment. For instance, if you aspire to be an artist, fill your space with art that inspires you, tools of the trade, and maybe even biographies of artists you admire.

Programming your RAS involves consistent, focused attention to your desired outcome. By repeatedly drawing your focus back to your goals through these exercises, you ensure that your brain constantly looks for ways to make them a reality.

Chapter 3
The Mind, The Body, and The Spirit

"A healthy person has a thousand
wishes. A sick person has only one."
~a well-known proverb

The three pillars of health and wellness are the mind, body, and spirit (soul). To be healthy in one, you must be healthy in all. In this book, we are programming the mind to achieve goals and dreams. To have a healthy mind, we must also work on the health of our body and spirit. We must recognize all of these pillars. Documented evidence shows a positive correlation between physical exercise and the cognitive functioning of the brain. (Mandolesi et al, 2018). Nutrition is also positively correlated with the cognitive function of the brain. Before one can be healthy, one must be right with one's spirituality. I'm not saying one must have religion, but one must find harmony with spirituality even if one believes in not believing in anything.

Dr. Stephan Covey is known for the 7 Habits of Highly Effective People book. The seventh habit, he calls Sharpen the Saw, refers to keeping your best tool sharp. You are that tool. He refers to the four areas of your life, the physical, social/emotional, mental, and spiritual. It would be best if you kept yourself sharp in these areas. Take care of your body by eating nutritious foods, exercising, and physical activity. My students recognize my mantra of diet, exercise, and sleep to treat and prevent disease and to be healthy. Humans are very social animals. It is unhealthy to keep secluded—schedule time with friends and family. Go out and meet new people and socialize. If you are an introvert, try to start a conversation with a friendly-looking stranger in a public place.

*"An investment in knowledge pays
the best interest."
~Benjamin Franklin*

The Mind

Feed your brain well. Nurturing your mind with positive knowledge is essential for anyone looking to make meaningful strides in personal and professional life. Books like this one "Start on Your Dreams," offer a structured 7-step process to goal achievement and serve as invaluable resources for those aiming to better themselves. Reading such material doesn't just offer actionable advice; it also encourages a mindset of constant learning and adaptability. This aligns with Step 1: Define Your Dreams, where equipping yourself with the right knowledge can help you crystallize what you truly aspire to achieve. Knowledgeable insights empower you to set specific, ambitious, and achievable goals, as stated in Step 2: Set Your Goals.

Online courses are another excellent avenue for personal development. In today's digital age, many resources are available at your fingertips, covering a wide array of topics from time management and financial literacy to emotional intelligence and leadership skills. These courses often provide theoretical knowledge, practical exercises, and real-world examples that help you translate what you've learned into actionable steps. Incorporating such learning experiences into your Massive Action Plan (Step 3) can significantly enhance the effectiveness of your strategies, giving you the tools needed to execute your plan successfully.

Furthermore, pursuing positive knowledge can be particularly crucial when you reach the stages of 'Fail and Pivot' (Step 6) and 'Execute Revised Plan' (Step 7). Failing is an inherent part of any path to success, but feeding your brain with constructive material helps build resilience and equips you with alternative strategies. Books, courses, and other educational resources can provide the tools to analyze your setbacks objectively, learn from them, and then pivot toward a more effective approach. In essence, continuously enriching your mind elevates your entire journey from dream definition to successful execution, making the road a little less bumpy and the destination much more attainable.

Meditation, an age-old practice embraced by cultures and traditions worldwide, is often misunderstood by many. One of the most common misconceptions about meditation is that it requires one to "empty" the mind completely. Meditation is more about training the mind to focus, rather than attempting to drive away all thoughts. This focused state of mind, achieved through meditation, offers many benefits, from reduced stress and anxiety to improved concentration and heightened self-awareness. The aim isn't to suppress thoughts but to observe them without judgment, achieving a calm and centered state of being.

The environment in which one meditates plays a significant role in the overall experience. To derive maximum benefits, it's important to set up a meditation space that is calming and free from distractions. Choose a quiet corner of your home where you won't be interrupted. This space should feel peaceful and be kept clean. Consider using soft cushions or a meditation mat for comfort. Incorporating gentle lighting, aromatic candles, or even subtle background sounds, like a babbling brook or soft chimes, can enhance your meditation experience. The key is creating a space where you feel relaxed and easily shift into a meditative state.

There are numerous meditation techniques designed to help train the mind's focus. Two such methods I like to use include the candlelight technique and the orange technique. In the candlelight technique, one focuses intently on the flame of a candle, observing its movement and brightness, and letting other thoughts fade away. Once the image of the candle's flame is embedded into your mind, close your eyes and keep that image alive. If the image starts to fade, open your eyes again to recapture the image. Keep repeating the cycle and then you will notice, after time, you will be able to keep the image alive in your mind for longer durations. This exercise helps in sharpening concentration.

On the other hand, the orange technique involves focusing on an object, such as an orange. Observing its texture, color, smell, and shape in detail allows the meditators to ground themselves in the present moment. Such techniques help hone concentration and facilitate a deeper connection with one's surroundings and the present moment.

Mindfulness is being fully present in the moment, keenly aware of yourself, your surroundings, and your reactions to the environment without judgment. It's about immersing yourself in the current experience, taking note of your feelings, thoughts, and bodily sensations. The beauty of mindfulness lies in its simplicity; it doesn't necessitate any elaborate rituals or practices. Instead, it encourages a heightened sense of awareness in everyday activities. With consistent practice, mindfulness can bring about a profound transformation in one's perspective, leading to greater clarity, understanding, and peace.

The benefits of practicing mindfulness are manifold and significant. It has been linked to reduced levels of stress, anxiety, and depression. Grounding individuals in the present, often curtails the spiraling of negative thoughts, thus fostering emotional regulation. Additionally, mindfulness has been shown to improve focus, concentration, and cognitive flexibility. Some research even suggests that mindfulness can lead to structural changes in the brain, particularly in attention and sensory processing areas.

Engaging in mindfulness activities can be a practical and enjoyable way to incorporate this practice into daily life. Activities such as mindful eating, where one savor every bite, recognizing its taste, texture, and aroma, can transform ordinary experiences into moments of deep awareness. Mindful walking, be it in a park or even within one's home, involves paying close attention to each step, feeling the ground beneath, and noticing the rhythm of one's breath. Simple daily tasks, like washing dishes or brushing teeth, can also become mindfulness practices when done with complete attention. These activities enhance the immediate experience and cultivate a habit of being present, ultimately contributing to overall well-being.

*"The person you will be in five
years depends largely on the information you feed your mind today. Be
picky about the books you read, the people you spend time with, and the conversations you engage in."*
~ *Ruben Chavez*

The Body

In my undergraduate classes at Arizona State University, I majored in kinesiology, which is the study of human movement, including exercise science. I have also studied nutrition and wellness, among several other subjects. To feed the brain and the body, one must exercise, eat right, and get enough sleep every night. Eating right does not mean a salad for every meal. Nutrition is all about balance. Getting a good variety of real food. The issue I have with the Standard American Diet (SAD) is all the fake food-like products we eat. I always say that if you eat the McFood, you'll get the McBody.

*"If you eat the McFood,
you'll get the McBody"*
~*Jerry Coy*

Navigating the expansive world of nutrition can be overwhelming, so I'll distill my advice succinctly: prioritize whole foods. One of the most visually appealing and nutritionally effective strategies I advocate for is "coloring your plate." This means incorporating a diverse range of fruits and vegetables of every hue. Each color often corresponds to specific nutrients, ensuring a well-rounded intake.

While there are many diets out there, each with its fervent proponents, I tend to gravitate towards what I've termed the "real food" approach. Essentially, it gets a thumbs up if it's a food you could pluck, gather, or hunt without excessive processing. Think of it as an evolved paleo approach, favoring foods in their natural state. My wife, for instance, has seen success with the Keto diet. While it's undeniable that many experience weight loss with Keto, I have reservations due to concerns over its high-fat focus. As always, finding what works for you is essential, bearing in mind long-term health implications, not just short-term gains.

Exercise Regularly for Brain Health

Regular physical exercise is not just beneficial for your body; it also has a significant impact on mental acuity. Cardiovascular exercises like walking, jogging, swimming, or cycling effectively boost brain function. These activities increase blood flow to the brain and help release neurochemicals like endorphins, natural mood lifters, and brain-derived neurotrophic factor (BDNF). This protein promotes the growth and maintenance of nerve cells. These effects improve cognitive functions like memory, attention, and problem-solving skills. Incorporating at least 150 minutes of moderate aerobic exercise into your weekly routine can help keep your mind sharp and may even delay cognitive decline as you age.

Strength training and flexibility exercises such as weightlifting and yoga also offer cognitive benefits. While the mechanisms aren't entirely understood, resistance training has been shown to improve aspects of cognitive function, including executive functions like planning and focusing. Yoga and similar mindfulness-based exercises improve physical flexibility and help reduce stress and mental clarity. The key is to create a balanced exercise regimen incorporating different forms of physical activities, allowing you to reap the most comprehensive benefits for both body and mind. Keeping the workouts varied can also make the exercise routine more engaging, contributing to mental sharpness.

The Spirit

Maintaining a healthy spirit is essential for overall well-being and can be achieved without adhering to a religious doctrine. One key element to nurturing a healthy spirit is mindfulness—being present in the moment. Practicing mindfulness through meditation or simply taking a few minutes each day to disconnect from the external world helps cultivate inner peace. This self-awareness enables you to recognize and manage your thoughts and emotions, fostering emotional resilience and clarity. By consistently spending time in a mindful state, you open a pathway to deeper self-understanding and a sense of unity with your surroundings, which are vital for spiritual health.

Another effective way to nourish the spirit is through meaningful connections with others. Building and maintaining relationships that offer emotional support, understanding, and shared values can be incredibly enriching. These connections don't have to be numerous; even one or two close relationships can profoundly impact your spiritual well-being. Compassion, empathy, and love, the foundations of any strong relationship, are spiritual qualities that help make life more fulfilling. Interactions with friends, family, or community members who bring positivity into your life can rejuvenate your spirit, giving you the strength to face life's challenges.

Lastly, finding purpose or meaning in life activities, even mundane ones, can fortify your spirit. Whether through work, hobbies, or volunteer efforts, engage in activities that make you feel like you are part of something larger than yourself. This could mean taking up a cause you're passionate about or setting personal goals that challenge you to grow. By focusing on what provides you with a sense of purpose, you create a narrative for your life that guides and enriches your spiritual self. While these activities may not be explicitly 'spiritual,' they can profoundly and uplift your state of being.

Chapter 4
The Right Mindset

"Whether you think you can or
you think you can't – you're right."
~Henry Ford

Before embarking on the transformative journey of the 7-step process in this book, it's necessary to purge negativity from your mental space. Negativity acts like a mental fog, clouding judgment, diluting focus, and hindering the mind's innate power to manifest dreams. Negative thoughts and emotions create mental barriers, derailing even the best-laid plans. These negative states must be recognized and dispelled, whether it's self-doubt, anxiety, or a general sense of pessimism. Think of it as mental decluttering; removing these obstructive elements creates a clear path for positive thinking, empowering your mind to attract and achieve what aligns with your dreams and goals.

In today's diverse and interconnected world, harboring feelings of hate, racism, homophobia, heterophobia, xenophobia, and similar prejudiced sentiments is not only morally reprehensible but also a significant hindrance to personal and collective progress. Such beliefs build barriers between individuals, preventing collaboration, under-standing, and mutual growth. More so, they also act as poison for the mind. When we cling to prejudice and allow these negative feelings to consume us, we limit our potential, hinder our ability to understand others, and stunt our emotional and cognitive growth. Beyond the harm caused to others, these sentiments corrode our mental well-be-ing, clouding our judgment, and distancing us from the core values of empathy, understanding, and unity. Embracing a mindset of ac-ceptance, inclusivity, and understanding, on the other hand, enhances our relationships with others and elevates our mental state, paving the way for personal and shared success.

Once you've cleared the mental fog of negativity, the next crucial step is to infuse your mindset with positivity. Think of your mind as fertile soil; having removed the weeds of negative thought, it's time to plant seeds of optimism, confidence, and resilience. Engage in af-firmations that reaffirm your capabilities and worth. Surround your-self with inspirational content, whether reading books like this one, "Start on Your Dreams," listening to uplifting podcasts, or engaging with motivational speakers. Fill your mental space with thoughts and images that serve your dreams, reminding yourself of your aspirations and the positive steps you can take to achieve them.

Being positive doesn't mean ignoring challenges or setbacks but viewing them as opportunities for growth and learning. A positive mindset is like a magnet for success and abundance, drawing them closer to you. This cultivated positivity makes the journey more en-joyable and supercharges your mind's manifesting power, enabling you to conceive and achieve your dreams more easily.

"Once you replace negative
thoughts with positive ones, you'll start
having positive results."
~ Willie Nelson

One of the most insidious barriers to achieving your dreams is the "poverty mindset"—a perspective rooted in scarcity and limitation rather than abundance and potential. This mindset often manifests as blame-shifting, where the responsibility for one's situation is placed on external factors or other people. While it's true that circumstances can be challenging, harboring a poverty mindset and blaming others perpetuate a cycle of inaction and defeat. Eradicating this outlook is vital to setting the stage for your 7-step journey outlined in this book.

It's not uncommon to encounter individuals who, instead of analyzing their circumstances or mindsets, point fingers at the successful, blaming them for their financial hardships. This "blame game" approach oversimplifies complex societal issues and perpetuates a victim mentality. It's essential to recognize that harboring resentment against the wealthy or successful is counterproductive. When we channel our energies into tearing someone else down, we waste precious time and effort that could have been used to elevate our circumstances. Moreover, by adopting such a perspective, we unknowingly stop ourselves from learning the strategies and mindsets these successful individuals employed to achieve success. Instead of resenting wealth, we should seek to understand the pathways to it, ensuring we don't trap ourselves in a cycle of bitterness and missed opportunities.

Instead of seeing what you don't have or can't do, focus on your assets and opportunities. Recognize that the power to change your circumstances begins within your mind. Stop blaming others for your setbacks; take ownership of your actions, plans, and future. By doing so, you shift from a reactive state to a proactive one—transitioning from being at the mercy of circumstances to being the architect of your destiny.

Replacing the poverty mindset with an abundance mindset empowers you to take control of your life. Doing so enables your mind's incredible manifesting power to operate at its full potential. You'll be better equipped to follow the 7-step process to its conclusion: realizing your dreams. The first step toward living the life you want is believing it's possible, which requires a mindset rich in positivity, responsibility, and limitless potential.

In pursuing your dreams, it's easy to fall into the trap of externalizing blame for your setbacks. The political climate, represented by parties like the Republicans or Democrats, often becomes a convenient scapegoat. While it's true that policy decisions can impact various aspects of life, attributing personal failures solely to political forces is a deflection that stifles personal growth. When you externalize blame in this way, you surrender your power and agency, effectively giving away control over your destiny.

The most empowering thing you can do is look in the mirror and acknowledge that the person staring back at you is responsible for your successes and failures. By taking full ownership of your life circumstances, you activate the immense power of your mind to bring about change. This personal accountability is a cornerstone of the 7-

step process described in this book, allowing you to navigate through each phase with a proactive, rather than reactive, mindset.

Remember, the power to manifest your dreams lies within you, not in the hands of politicians or external conditions. By focusing on what you can control and taking responsibility for your actions, you empower yourself to create the circumstances you desire, regardless of the political landscape. Your mindset becomes one of constructive action and self-reliance, key ingredients in the potent mix that transforms dreams into reality.

"Looking inside-out" is an empowering perspective that centers on self-examination before external blame. When something goes wrong—or even when it goes right—the first place to search for answers is within yourself. By looking inward, you take stock of your actions, choices, and mindset, the factors most directly under your control. This self-assessment gives you valuable insights into what you could do differently or continue doing to influence outcomes. Practicing an inside-out perspective is integral to the 7-step process, as it reinforces personal accountability and the proactive shaping of your destiny.

This principle is not just beneficial for individual growth; it's also transformative in relationships. Often, the instinctive reaction to conflict or dissatisfaction in relationships is to cast blame outward. However, if you first look inside-out, evaluating your behavior, communication, and contributions to the situation, you open the door to constructive dialogue and mutual growth. This approach can diffuse tension and lead to more meaningful, honest interactions. It allows both parties to address issues as allies in problem-solving rather than opponents in a blame game, strengthening the relationship and providing a solid foundation for shared dreams and goals.

In the tapestry of my own life, my relationship with my wife stands out as a testament to the power of looking "inside out." We share a bond that, for the most part, is harmonious and filled with mutual respect and understanding. Yet, on the rare occasions when disagreements arise, I often find that it's a result of my failure to look "inside-out." Instead of understanding her perspective or examining my internal emotions and triggers, I sometimes react based on external cues or immediate emotions. These moments are stark reminders of how vital it is to always approach situations, especially those closest to our hearts, from a reflective stance. By continually cultivating an "inside-out" perspective, we can enhance our relationships and foster deeper understanding and empathy for those we love.

"The only person who would turn my life around was me. The only way I could get turned around was to put myself through the worst things possible that a human being could ever endure."
~David Goggins

David Goggins, a former Navy SEAL and ultra-endurance athlete, champions the "Accountability Mirror" concept as a tool for personal growth and self-improvement. The idea is simple yet profound: when you look at yourself in the mirror, you face the one person you cannot lie to. Goggins encourages people to use this moment of reflection to confront their weaknesses, acknowledge their failures, and take responsibility for their actions. By doing so, you cut through self-deception and external blame, establishing a level of accountability that becomes the bedrock for meaningful change. This practice aligns well with the principles of the 7-step process in this book, emphasizing the importance of self-accountability in the journey towards making your dreams a reality.

David Goggins also introduces the "calloused mind" concept as a metaphor for building mental toughness and resilience. According to Goggins, just as one can develop physical calluses by repeatedly exposing skin to friction, a person can develop a calloused mind by frequently facing and overcoming challenges, adversity, and uncomfortable situations. This hardened mental state equips you to deal with life's difficulties more effectively and keeps you focused on your goals. Goggins argues that a calloused mind enables you to push past perceived limitations, confront your weaknesses, and take responsibility for your actions. The calloused mind is thus an essential tool in the 7-step process outlined in this book, helping you remain resilient through each phase, from defining your dreams to executing your revised plans.

Social media can be a double-edged sword. While it provides a platform for connection and knowledge-sharing, it can also be a breeding ground for negativity and distraction. The constant stream of content, ranging from inflammatory political debates to endless celebrity gossip, can easily pull you off course from your objectives. In the context of the 7-step process detailed in this book, it's essential to be mindful of social media's impact on your mindset and focus. The old computing adage "garbage in, garbage out" applies here. If you consume harmful or useless content, your thoughts and actions will reflect that, hindering your progress toward achieving your dreams.

The first step in surviving social media is to curate your feed. Unfollow accounts that constantly post harmful or distracting content. Instead, opt for profiles that inspire you, align with your goals, or provide valuable information that propels you further. The aim is to transform your social media platforms into a source of inspiration and knowledge rather than a black hole of procrastination and negativity. Remember, every moment spent scrolling aimlessly is a moment not spent actively working on your Massive Action Plan from Step 3.

Another essential strategy is to set boundaries for social media usage. Designate specific times for checking your platforms and stick to them. Use tools or apps that limit your social media use after a certain period. By controlling your interaction with these platforms, you empower yourself to use social media as a tool rather than letting it use you. By being mindful about what you consume online, you not only avoid the pitfalls of negativity but also preserve the integrity of your mental space, enabling you to stay aligned with your 7-step journey to manifesting your dreams.

Taking control of your digital environment is vital to maintaining focus and positivity. I deliberately decided to unfollow all news and political pages on social media platforms. While staying informed is necessary, the constant bombardment of breaking news and political debates cluttered my mind and distracted me from my goals. In addition to curating my feed, I also turned off all social media push notifications. This simple action shifted the power dynamic between me and my phone; instead of allowing my device to dictate my attention with every beep and buzz, I now choose when to engage with social media. This aligns perfectly with Step 3: Massive Action Plan, allowing me to allocate my time and mental energy towards activities directly contributing to achieving my dreams, as outlined in this book's 7-step process.

Multitasking is often touted as a valuable skill, especially in fast-paced, high-demand environments. However, what needs to be more commonly understood is that multitasking doesn't necessarily equate to effectiveness and can be counterproductive. Research indicates that when you multitask, you're not performing multiple tasks simultaneously but rapidly switching your focus from one task to another. This constant switching drains mental energy and increases time to complete each task. Moreover, each switch carries the risk of error, leading to sloppier work and diminished quality.

In the context of the 7-step process in this book, multitasking can be a severe impediment to achieving your dreams. Each step, from defining your dreams to executing your revised plan, requires a laser-like focus for optimal results. When you're juggling multiple tasks at once, you need to give every element of your plan the attention and quality it deserves. As you navigate through the steps, your Massive Action Plan can suffer if it's just one of many things you're trying to juggle simultaneously. Sloppy work won't just delay your progress; it can also have long-term consequences on your dream's viability.

So, instead of priding yourself on being a multitasker, aim to become an exceptional "single-tasker." Prioritize your tasks in alignment with your goals and give your undivided attention to each one in its turn. This way, you're more likely to produce higher quality and efficient work, getting you one step closer to making your dreams a reality. Remember, the key to achieving big dreams is not to scatter your attention across many things but to focus intently on each aspect of your plan.

In the journey toward making your dreams a reality, as outlined by the 7-step process in this book, the right mindset is not just an optional asset; it's a critical necessity. It all starts with purging negativity from your life, whether it emanates from your social media feed, immediate environment, or even within. This first step frees you from the mental barriers that often thwart progress before it even begins. Once you've created a clean slate, filling it with positivity becomes your next mission. Positive reinforcement through selective social media use, optimistic autosuggestions, and a focus on constructive actions set the stage for the following Massive Action Plan.

Equally important is eliminating the victim mindset that can quickly sabotage your best efforts. In a world where it's convenient to point fingers at political affiliations, society, or other external factors, the power to change lies within you. Looking "inside-out" helps you take ownership of your failures and successes. This level of self-accountability is necessary for effective problem-solving and navigating through the inevitable challenges you will face. Adopting principles like David Goggins' "Accountability Mirror" or fostering a "calloused mind" will help you survive and thrive in your journey.

The right mindset can be visualized as fertile soil, a nurturing environment where the seeds of your dreams and aspirations can sprout, grow, and eventually bloom. Renowned spiritual teacher Eckhart Tolle underscores the immense power of the present moment. We harness an unparalleled force that drives our ambitions when we anchor ourselves in the now with a mindful and positive outlook. This aligns perfectly with the essence of cultivating the right mindset.

Whether you find yourself in the initial stages of defining your dreams or you're deep into executing your revised plan, your mental state will predominantly determine the pace and direction of your journey. By actively sweeping away the cobwebs of negativity, welcoming beams of positivity, focusing with unwavering determination, and holding oneself accountable, the path through the 7-step process becomes not only clearer but also more navigable.

Start On Your Dreams

Chapter 5
Living in the Present

---

*"Realize deeply that the present
moment is all you have. Make the NOW
the primary focus of your life."*
~Eckhart Tolle

Eckhart Tolle, a profound spiritual teacher and bestselling author, has always emphasized the transformative power of living in the present. In his seminal work, "The Power of Now," Tolle elucidates how most of our anxieties, fears, and stresses emanate from either ruminating on the past or anxiously anticipating the future. By grounding ourselves in the present moment, we free ourselves from these self-imposed chains, allowing us to engage with life as it unfolds fully. Tolle's teachings remind us that the present is all we truly have, and by anchoring our awareness in the now, we can achieve a deeper sense of peace, clarity, and purpose.

"Realize deeply that the present moment is all you ever have. Make the Now the primary focus of your life."
–Eckhart Tolle

Living in the present, or being mindful of the "now," is not just a fleeting trend; it's a foundational aspect of many spiritual and philosophical traditions. The essence of this idea has been captured most eloquently in contemporary times by Eckhart Tolle in his seminal work, "The Power of Now." A recent social media trend is calling it the Art of Noticing. But why is being present so significant, and how does it relate to achieving success?

The Illusion of Past and Future

Human minds are conditioned to dwell either in the past, ruminating over things that have already happened, or in the future, with anticipation or anxiety about what's yet to come. These mental patterns can be seductive, often causing us to overlook the present. However, the past is but a collection of memories, and the future remains a realm of imagination. The only moment where life truly unfolds, where action can be taken, and where experiences can be genuinely felt, is the present.

Being in the present doesn't mean neglecting the lessons from the past or forgoing planning for the future. It means engaging wholeheartedly with the current moment, where actions and decisions shape future outcomes. When we are fully present, our senses are more acute, our responses more apt, and our actions more purposeful. By grounding ourselves in the present, we avoid being swept up in unnecessary worries or regrets, freeing up mental and emotional energy.

The journey through the 7-step process is best navigated when one is anchored in the present. When defining dreams, the passion felt in the current moment provides clarity. Setting goals requires an understanding of one's present situation. Acting, pivoting from failures, or revising plans are all processes that demand undivided attention to the here and now.

Moreover, the challenges and obstacles faced along the path of achieving dreams often arise from our reactions to past failures or anxieties about potential future setbacks. By focusing on the present moment, we can tackle these challenges with a clear mind, making decisions based on current circumstances rather than being influenced by past regrets or future fears.

"I've always got to where I'm going by walking away from where I've been."
~Winnie the Pooh (A.A. Milne)

Techniques to Stay Present

Mindfulness Meditation: A practice where one focuses on the breath, bodily sensations, or a specific mantra to anchor the mind in the present.

Gratitude Journals: Daily reflection on aspects of life one is grateful for can shift focus from what's lacking or uncertain to what's abundant and concrete in the now.

Limit Multitasking: Engage in one task at a time, immersing fully in each activity.

Digital Detox: Reducing screen time, especially from social media, can limit distractions and increase present-moment awareness.

Nature Walks: Spending time in nature, away from the bustle of modern life, can be grounding and help in attuning to the present.

Living in the present is not just a philosophical or spiritual concept but a necessary principle for those on the path to success. By anchoring ourselves in the now, we enhance our capacity to navigate life's challenges, make effective decisions, and progress steadily toward our dreams. As Tolle reminds us, the present moment is truly all we have, and harnessing its power is key to unlocking our potential.

Chapter 6
Routines and Habits

The importance of good habits and routines cannot be overstated when it comes to the journey of making your dreams a reality, as detailed in the 7-step process of this book. Much like the foundation of a building, habits, and routines serve as the underlying structure upon which your dreams are built. While a Massive Action Plan provides the roadmap, habits, and routines are the vehicle that transports you to your destination. They transform abstract concepts like ambition and potential into tangible results through consistent, daily actions.

Just as a river gradually carves a canyon, your habits—no matter how small—accumulate and result in monumental changes over time. They free up cognitive bandwidth, allowing your mind to focus on higher-level tasks such as decision-making and problem-solving. Routines, essentially a structured set of habits, bring predictability and discipline into your life, helping you manage your time and energy more effectively. In doing so, you set the stage for a fulfilling journey through each step, from defining your dreams to revising and executing your plans.

In the following chapter, we'll explore not just the mechanics of habit formation but also how you can tailor your habits to align seamlessly with each step in your journey toward achieving your dreams. Good habits and routines are not mere lifestyle choices; they're fundamental tools for anyone serious about transforming their dreams into reality.

"You do not rise to the level of your goals. You fall to the level of your systems." ~James Clear

"Atomic Habits" by James Clear is a bestselling book that delves into the science of habits and how tiny changes can lead to remarkable results in your life. Lays out a framework for understanding how habits work and provides practical strategies to break bad habits and build good ones. Using a combination of scientific research, real-world examples, and storytelling, the book emphasizes the power of compound growth, illustrating how small, incremental changes can snowball into significant transformation over time.

In summary, "Atomic Habits" offers a comprehensive guide to understanding the mechanics of habit formation and change. James Clear articulates that it's not necessarily the magnitude of the change that matters, but the consistency and accumulation of small improvements that lead to lasting results. This concept resonates strongly with the 7-step process detailed in this book, especially when it comes to implementing a Massive Action Plan. Incorporating good habits into your routine will pave a smoother path toward achieving your dreams.

Jerry Coy

Stephen Covey's "The 7 Habits of Highly Effective People" is a seminal work in the self-help genre, offering a principle-centered approach to solving personal and professional problems. Covey outlines seven habits that encourage individuals to move from dependence to independence and ultimately towards interdependence, which is effective cooperation with others. These habits range from proactivity and setting end goals ("Begin with the End in Mind") to prioritizing important tasks ("Put First Things First"). The later habits focus on interpersonal effectiveness and continuous improvement, encapsulating concepts like "Think Win-Win," "Seek First to Understand, then to be Understood," "Synergize," and "Sharpen the Saw." The book posits that by internalizing and implementing these habits, one can achieve a high level of effectiveness and fulfillment.

The importance of establishing good habits and routines cannot be emphasized enough, especially when you consider their compounding effects over time. Like a snowball rolling downhill, the benefits of good habits multiply, creating positive outcomes that far outweigh the initial efforts required to establish them. These habits lay the foundation for success in any endeavor, whether it's personal development, career growth, or achieving life goals. Small, consistent actions lead to significant, long-lasting results; the sooner you start, the sooner you'll reap the benefits.

Starting early is key. Just as compound interest amplifies the growth of an investment, the advantages of good habits amplify over time, too. When you invest in yourself through good habits and routines, you invest in your future self. The dividends paid regarding health, well-being, and success can be monumental. This is why it is crucial to build these habits and routines early on. Each day you stick to a good habit, you're taking one step closer to your ultimate goals, and the compounded returns of your consistent efforts will ultimately lead to a life of greater fulfillment and achievement.

"You will never change your life until you change something you do daily. The secret of your success is found in your daily routine."
~Darren Hardy

In the transformative book, The Compound Effect, Darren Hardy illustrates the profound impact of daily routines and the consistent, minor steps we can employ to achieve remarkable success. At its core, Hardy's principle teaches us that everyday decisions, not just monumental ones, shape our destiny. Over time, these small, deliberate choices compound, guiding us toward our aspirations or away from them. This foundational concept of small actions leading to significant outcomes finds its echo in our 7-step system.

My 7-step framework isn't just a set of stages but a practical embodiment of the Compound Effect in action. From crystallizing dreams and setting tangible goals to devising actionable plans and adapting when faced with setbacks, the emphasis is firmly on consistency and diligence. By marrying the daily intentional choices with the structure of these seven steps, we harness the power of the Compound Effect, letting it work in our favor. Through this, the 7-step system becomes more than a guide; it is a deliberate strategy to ensure our daily endeavors align seamlessly with our broader vision, ultimately paving the way to our goals. As we delve deeper into each

Jerry Coy

step, you'll witness how they act as the building blocks, magnifying the impact of our daily decisions to shape our desired future.

Successful individuals' daily habits and routines often serve as cornerstones of their achievements. These structured behaviors practiced consistently, can compound over time, driving unparalleled results.

In 2014, Admiral William H. McRaven delivered a powerful commencement speech at the University of Texas at Austin, emphasizing the profound impact of small, daily routines on one's life. He said, "If you want to change the world, start by making your bed. If you make your bed every morning, you will have accomplished the day's first task. It will give you a small sense of pride and encourage you to do another task and another and another. By the end of the day, that one task completed will have turned into many tasks completed. Making your bed will also reinforce the fact that little things in life matter." This sentiment, which later became the foundation of McRaven's bestselling book, underscores the significance of cultivating positive habits and routines. By mastering the small tasks, we lay the groundwork for greater achievements and foster a mindset that prioritizes discipline, order, and perseverance.

The "Hour of Power" is a transformative concept popularized by life coach and self-help guru Tony Robbins. The idea emphasizes the importance of dedicating the first hour of your day to personal growth and setting a positive and proactive tone for the hours to come. Robbins' "Hour of Power" is divided into four 15-minute segments: visualization, reading, journaling, and exercise. This structure is designed to stimulate the mind, body, and spirit, ensuring you're mentally, physically, and emotionally equipped to take on the challenges of the day. While the notion of devoting time to self-improvement isn't new,

Tony Robbins' distinct approach to the "Hour of Power" has inspired countless individuals to reshape their mornings and, by extension, their lives.

To effectively implement your "Hour of Power," begin by setting a consistent wake-up time that allows you to have this undisturbed hour before diving into your daily tasks. Start with 15 minutes of visualization: imagine your goals, dream vividly and feel the emotions tied to those achievements. Then, allocate the next 15 minutes to read – this could be a motivational book, a self-help guide, or any literature that fuels your personal growth. The following 15-minute segment is for journaling. Write down your thoughts, express gratitude, or detail your aspirations. Putting pen to paper can bring clarity and cement intentions. Finally, spend the last 15 minutes engaging in a physical activity. Whether it's stretching, a quick workout, or even a brisk walk, the idea is to awaken your body. Over time, this structured hour will become a cherished ritual, grounding you and preparing you to seize each day.

Take Steve Jobs, the iconic co-founder of Apple. Every day, he wore the same black turtleneck, blue jeans, and New Balance sneakers. This wasn't just a fashion statement; it was a conscious decision to eliminate the burden of choice in his daily routine. By reducing decision fatigue, Jobs could channel his cognitive resources into more critical areas of thinking, such as product development and innovation. His routine of uniform dressing enabled him to maintain mental clarity and focus on the tasks that truly mattered.

Then there's Oprah Winfrey, one of the most influential figures in the media. Beyond her on-screen prowess, Oprah's morning routine has been vital to her success. She starts her day with meditation,

Jerry Coy

grounding herself, and setting an intention for the day. This practice is followed by a rigorous exercise regimen, boosting her energy and promoting mental clarity. By nurturing her mind and body first thing every morning, Oprah ensures she's primed for the challenges and opportunities.

Bill Gates, co-founder of Microsoft, is known for his voracious reading habits. He attributes a significant portion of his success and knowledge to his routine of reading daily. Every night, regardless of how late it is or where he is, Gates spends at least an hour reading a book, ranging from non-fiction to scientific journals. This habit not only broadens his perspective but also fosters continuous learning, a trait synonymous with many successful entrepreneurs.

In essence, these examples underscore a vital truth: success isn't just a product of inherent talent or occasional bursts of effort. Instead, it's often the outcome of daily habits and routines, practiced with dedication and consistency over time. These structured behaviors, seemingly minor when viewed in isolation, can compound, paving the way for monumental achievements.

In today's fast-paced world, it's easy to become overwhelmed by the sheer volume of tasks and responsibilities one must manage. Distractions are omnipresent, and the allure of instant gratification often overshadows the discipline required to maintain consistency. However, as seen through the examples of luminaries such as Steve Jobs, Oprah Winfrey, and Bill Gates, success is a deliberate choice, manifested through disciplined routines and unwavering habits. These individuals only achieved their monumental successes over time. Instead, they meticulously crafted their days, months, and years around routines that optimized their potential.

Furthermore, these routines and habits aren't solely reserved for the likes of billionaires and media moguls. Anyone can adopt and integrate them into their daily lives. It begins with a simple commitment to oneself, recognizing the immense power habits wield, and then nurturing these habits until they become second nature. When combined with the 7-step process highlighted in this book, these habits serve as the gears in the well-oiled machine that is your journey towards realizing your dreams.

The road to success is paved with the bricks of daily habits and routines. Each brick represents a choice, a decision to prioritize long-term growth over short-term convenience. As we've explored, these choices, no matter how insignificant they may seem in the moment, compound over time, shaping our destiny. Our 7-step process is a testament to this, emphasizing the necessity of integrating habits into our daily lives to ensure the realization of our dreams. Embrace the power of routines, recognize the potential of consistent, incremental progress, and watch as your aspirations transform from mere dreams to tangible realities. Remember, it's not the grand gestures but the daily disciplines, that dictate the trajectory of our lives.

Chapter 7
Don't Settle for Average

"Perfection is not attainable, but if we chase perfection, we can catch excellence."
~Vince Lombardi

In a world characterized by vast opportunities and boundless potential, it's a tragedy that so many choose to tread the path of mediocrity. Somewhere along the way, many of us have been conditioned to believe that "good enough" is an acceptable standard and that doing just enough to get by is the way to navigate life. This seemingly harmless mindset robs us of our potential and the splendors of life when we truly engage with passion and purpose.

The reality is that average has become a comfortable safety net for many. But in this safety lies stagnation, the antithesis of growth and progress. By quietly quitting—by doing the minimum required, by not fully committing or engaging—we not only do a disservice to those around us but, more crucially, to ourselves. We silently accept that we are not meant for greater things, slowly extinguishing the inner flame that once drove us to dream big.

This chapter is a clarion call to break free from the shackles of mediocrity. It's an invitation to challenge the status quo, to reach beyond what's comfortable, and to excel in all facets of life truly. Excellence isn't about being the best in the world but being the best for the world and yourself. Embrace the journey of relentless improvement, shed the weight of complacency, and dive into why you should never settle for average.

> *"It's okay to be normal; just try not to be average."*
> *~Jerry Coy*

In my classroom, I've witnessed brilliance masked by complacency. Bright minds settle for a mere 'C' when excellence is within reach. Beyond imparting knowledge, I see my role as a catalyst, igniting the dormant spark within these students. Every Monday, I initiated a 'TGIM' session—Thank God It's Monday, an idea inspired by the fervor of ET the Hip Hop Preacher. Through invigorating activities, we explored our purpose, delved into transformative books like Cal Newport's "So Good They Can't Ignore You," and harnessed the power of journaling to uncover and commit to our deepest 'whys'.

In the realm of career advice, Cal Newport offers a refreshing, contrarian perspective with his book "So Good They Can't Ignore You." Dissecting the oft-repeated mantra of "follow your passion," Newport posits that passion comes *after* mastery. Instead of pursuing a relentless quest for an elusive "dream job," Newport suggests honing your skills to the point of excellence in whatever you do. Becoming indispensable in your field creates career capital, giving you the leverage to pursue meaningful and fulfilling work. His thesis emphasizes the significance of craftsmanship, continual learning, and striving for excellence, steering away from average achievements.

"Your work is going to fill a large part of your life, and the only way to be truly satisfied is to do what you believe is great work. And the only way to do great work is to love what you do. If you haven't found it yet, keep looking. Don't settle. As with all matters of the heart, you'll know when you find it."

~ Steve Jobs

You've taken the first step by picking up this book, signaling your readiness to embark on a transformative journey. Feel the power within you, the hunger to rise above mediocrity. Take a moment. Breathe deeply. Now, with conviction, declare, "I am destined for greatness!" Bid farewell to the habits that hold you back and embrace those that propel you forward. Mastery over your time awaits; let it amplify your efficiency and productivity. The path to your dreams begins now, not on some distant Monday or in a new year. Seize this moment, for greatness lies within your grasp. Carpe diem!

Embarking on the path to greatness is a deliberate choice that begins with understanding oneself. It's essential first to look inward and take stock of who you are—your strengths, weaknesses, passions, and fears. This deep introspection lays the groundwork for the journey ahead. Recognizing areas where you've settled for mediocrity and feeling the burning desire for change is the first step toward a life of excellence.

Once this self-awareness is cultivated, the next phase involves crystallizing your vision. Greatness is not an ambiguous concept; clear, purposeful goals sculpt it. Envisioning where you want to be, the pinnacle you aspire to reach acts as the North Star guiding you through the tumultuous seas of life's challenges.

But it's not enough to dream; one must act fervently. Action, driven by unwavering commitment and passion, bridges the realm of dreams and reality. Take calculated risks, embrace failures as learning opportunities, and persistently refine your strategies. Surround yourself with like-minded individuals, mentors, and guides who can share their wisdom and insights.

Remember, the path to greatness is not a sprint but a marathon. It demands resilience, patience, and an unyielding spirit. Every day is an opportunity to learn, grow, and inch closer to the version of yourself you've always envisioned. By embracing this journey with an open heart and a determined mind, the horizon of greatness isn't just a distant dream but a tangible future waiting to be realized.

Navigating the path to greatness isn't just about knowing which steps to take but also about recognizing the pitfalls that might divert your course or stall your progress. One of the most insidious challenges people face on this journey is succumbing to various addictions, whether they're related to substances, technology, or even toxic patterns of thought. These addictive behaviors can numb one's senses and distract from the clarity of purpose, leading to a life lived in the shadows of potential rather than the brilliance of achievement.

In addition to personal vices, the company one keeps can profoundly influence the trajectory toward excellence. Bad relationships or friendships can act like anchors, weighing down aspirations with negativity, doubt, and distractions. They often breed complacency, making the comfort zone appear far more appealing than the uncertain road ahead. The comfort zone, while cozy and familiar, is a silent dream killer. It's where aspirations stagnate and visions blur, leaving greatness as just another unattained fantasy.

To steer clear of these pitfalls, one must be both vigilant and proactive. Regular self-reflection can help identify and address budding addictions or toxic patterns before they take root. Foster relationships with individuals who share your vision or, at the very least, understand and respect your journey. Such individuals can offer valuable support, guidance, and accountability. Finally, continuously challenge yourself. Set milestones that force you out of your comfort zone and celebrate each victory, no matter how small. Staying alert and committed makes the path to greatness less fraught with peril and more laden with promise.

J.K. Rowling was once an unemployed single mother struggling to make ends meet. She faced numerous rejections when trying to get her first book, "Harry Potter and the Philosopher's Stone," published.

Many publishers couldn't see the potential in her tale of a young wizard. Despite the setbacks, Rowling believed in her story and didn't let the rejections deter her. Her unwavering faith in her work and her resilience in the face of adversity eventually led to her manuscript being accepted by Bloomsbury Publishing. From there, the "Harry Potter" series took off, selling hundreds of millions of copies worldwide, turning into a blockbuster film franchise, and making Rowling one of the wealthiest authors in the world. Her journey emphasizes the importance of perseverance, belief in oneself, and the idea that greatness often comes from the most unexpected beginnings.

In previous chapters, we delved into the transformative potential of cultivating the right mindset. Train your mind to not just seek growth, but to chase after greatness relentlessly. As we venture into subsequent chapters, we'll unravel the invaluable role of failures. Rather than setbacks, envision them as milestones on your road to excellence, teaching you invaluable lessons. If ever duped out of money, reframe the loss as tuition paid for a crucial life lesson. Your journey to greatness is paved with experiences, both good and challenging. Embrace them all.

True greatness is a deeply personal endeavor, not a race against others. Each of us walks a unique path, shaped by distinct experiences, challenges, and dreams. While our journeys might intersect or run parallel at times, they are never identical. Comparing our progress to someone else's can cloud our vision, sidelining our potential. Understanding that being the best version of oneself doesn't mean settling is essential. Even as you excel in your light, always harbor the ambition to be the GOAT (Greatest of All Time). In this vast tapestry of life, your thread should be woven with the vibrancy of your personal best, shining brightly, irrespective of those around you.

In the grand journey of life, each of us is endowed with the potential for greatness. It's not about simply surpassing others in a race to the top, but about delving deep within, acknowledging our inherent strengths, and nurturing them to their zenith. We've explored the pitfalls that can divert us, the attitudes that can elevate us, and the inspiration that can drive us. Remember, genuine greatness is not about fleeting moments of fame or temporary triumphs. It's about the legacy you create the positive impact you make, and the life you lead, with passion, purpose, and an unwavering commitment to excellence. Rise above the ordinary, break free from the shackles of mediocrity, and let your journey be one of unparalleled greatness.

Unit 2
The 7 Steps to Success

Programming Your Brain to Make Dreams Come True

Step 1   Define your Dreams

Step 2   Set Your Goals

Step 3   Massive Action Plan

Step 4   Assemble Your Team

Step 5   Execute Plan

Step 6   Fail and Pivot

Step 7   Execute Revised Plan

Chapter 8
My Early Dream

*"Damn the torpedoes, full speed
ahead!"*
~*Admiral David Glasgow Farragut*

Way back when I was still a boy, I loved watching movies about ships and naval battles, some of my favorites include The Sea Wolf with Edward G. Robinson (1941), *Mutiny on the Bounty, Mr. Roberts* with Henry Fonda, and Tora! Tora! Tora! (1970) and *Midway* from 1976. I remember seeing Midway in the theater because it was the second of only four movies with "Sensurround-Sound," where they installed special speakers in the theater. I also enjoyed Shows like McHale's Navy with Ernest Borgnine. Because of my love of ships and Navy tradition, my dream was to serve in the U.S. Navy.

During high school, I was a chubby child who struggled with fitness. During my senior year in high school, I did not qualify to serve in the Navy. At the time, I had to weigh less than 205 pounds according to my height. I exceeded the maximum by well over 25 pounds. I wanted to join by the beginning of the summer after I turned 18 years old. So around February before the summer, I decided to accept the challenge to lose weight.

At that time, I had yet to develop my 7-steps, but I do remember using several of the elements of my plan to succeed with the challenge. In my bedroom, I would hang Navy recruiting posters and similar photos to keep me motivated. It also reminds me of my goal. Sometimes dieters will forget they're dieting until after an unhealthy meal. So, the first step of my 7-steps is to define what your dreams are and find a "why". I accomplished this step along with the visual cues that you will learn about in the next chapter "Define Your Dreams.".

After defining dreams, one must set goals. You may ask yourself "What's the difference?" Dreams are broader and goals are narrower. Goals are more specific and more actionable. I will discuss greater detail about goals in the chapter "Set Your Goals." When I set my goal, it was very specific. I had to lose at least 25 pounds before the end of May. It was an ambitious yet realistic goal. I had a measurable number and a timeframe. These are very important elements of setting goals. Most importantly, I wrote down this goal.

After I had set my goal, I needed an "Action Plan". The first step established my 'why', the second step established my 'what', and now I needed a 'how'. I was only 18 and I didn't know nearly as much about nutrition or fitness as I do now. Okay, one may say I knew almost nothing about them. My Action Plan would be considered quite unhealthy, and I do not recommend it at all. I planned to eat only 3 cans of condensed soup per day and drink a lot of water. This was an extremely tough diet and not sustainable at all. Maintaining my motivation was difficult, to say the least. My motivational posters and written plans kept me going.

So long story short, I did lose weight and I joined the Navy right after high school; however, I was weakened by the unhealthy method of weight loss. During my Navy physical, my blood pressure was extremely low; around 80 over 50. Days before my weigh-in physical, I would use the sauna to lose water weight and dehydrate. Please do not do as I did. I also should have worked on my physical endurance with exercise. After arriving at basic training aka Boot Camp, the physical demands were another challenge. In addition to the push-ups and sit-ups, I was required to complete a one-and-a-half-mile run within thirteen minutes.

My lack of fitness and nutrition knowledge back then made it way more challenging than it needed to be. My theory at the time was that if I lost more weight, then I would be lighter; and if I'm lighter, then push-ups, sit-ups, and running would be easier. It made perfect sense at the time. The problem was that during basic training, I would continue my starvation diet. The inadequate protein intake would prevent my muscles from recovering after physical training. I did lose a lot of weight, but my fitness level was not adapting well.

I did get through basic training, and I even made that run in the time required. The only reason was because of a five-hour on-base liberty with my parents. They went with me to the enlisted club where I had a pizza for lunch, and we went back for a steak dinner. All that protein and carbohydrates gave me so much energy, I performed considerably better on Monday morning. After I got set back a week in training, I changed my strategy at Chow (mess hall). I ate food, especially protein. A few days later I was able to complete my physical fitness test and graduated basic training the next day.

I initially failed the Navy physical fitness test. There was even talk of giving me an airplane ticket home. I pleaded with them to let me stay because serving in the Navy was a childhood dream. Step 6 of my system is to Fail and Pivot. I failed. Once I identified the reason for my failure was my poor diet, I pivoted. Instead of giving up, I executed my revised plan by changing my diet and continuing to train. It paid off since I was able to succeed in my fitness test.

From childhood, a fervent passion for naval movies and shows ingrained a dream within me to serve in the U.S. Navy. However, the journey towards realizing this dream was fraught with challenges. My high school years were marked by weight issues that rendered me ineligible for the Navy based on the set fitness standards. Without the benefit of the structured 7-step system I would later develop, I utilized rudimentary versions of some of these steps. I defined my dream, reinforced it with visual cues, and set a specific weight loss goal. My initial action plan was markedly flawed, stemming from limited knowledge of nutrition and fitness. This unhealthy diet led to significant weight loss, but also to physical weakness. Once in the Navy's basic training, the physical demands compounded the challenge. My initial failure in the Navy physical fitness test was a turning point, pushing me to pivot, make dietary changes, and fortify my training routine.

My journey to join the Navy underscored the importance of each step in my eventual 7-step system. Dreams need definition, and goals require specificity. Action plans should be informed by proper knowledge, and when one encounters failure, the ability to pivot is invaluable. My experience serves as a testament to the effectiveness of these steps. Although I made missteps due to the lack of a structured system, the essence of my eventual 7-step plan was already in play. This tale not only reflects the significance of determination and adaptability but also underscores the importance of knowledge and informed planning in achieving one's dreams. It's a narrative that demonstrates the concept of 'Fail and Pivot' in action, showing that failures can be transformed into stepping-stones with the right mindset and approach.

Reflecting on my journey, I realize that the path to fulfilling a childhood dream is never a straight line. Throughout our lives, each of us encounters various challenges, both expected and unexpected. What separates a success story from a tale of missed opportunities is one's determination to adapt, pivot, and recalibrate when faced with these hurdles. My pursuit to join the Navy, despite several setbacks, stands as a testament to this relentless spirit. Driven by passion and maintained through sheer will, my story epitomizes the essence of perseverance.

Yet, this journey wasn't just about passion and tenacity. It also highlighted the undeniable value of preparation and informed decision-making. While my fervor gave me the drive, the initial lack of a systematic approach and thorough knowledge sometimes became barriers. This teaches an invaluable lesson: while dreams and determination are foundational, they must be paired with solid strategies and actionable knowledge. A dream might set the direction, and passion can fuel the journey, but knowledge ensures we remain on the right track.

My aspiration to join the Navy serves dual purposes: an inspiring testament to the resilience of the human spirit and a reminder of the importance of meticulous preparation. It emphasizes the ability to adapt to challenging situations and the significance of holding fast to one's dreams. However, it's equally a lesson on the importance of being prepared and having a well-charted plan in place, accentuating the advantages of a systematic approach like the 7-step method I've outlined. As you, the readers, embark on your unique quests, let my story serve as guidance, illuminating both the challenges to prepare for and the strategies to employ. With dreams, determination, the right plan, and adaptability, success is not just a possibility; it's a guarantee.

Chapter 9
Step 1 - Define Your Dreams

Finding Your "WHY"

"The future belongs to those who believe in the beauty of their dreams."
~Eleanor Roosevelt

Many life coaches will tell you to set your goals, write them down, and be persistent. They are skipping this most critical step. Before you can set a goal, you must establish exactly what you want and, most importantly, why you want it. If you don't define your dreams first, you may work toward the wrong goals. First, ask yourself, "What do I want in my life?" That sounds easy enough, but we need to probe further. For this, you will need to write down some stuff. I recommend you use a composition book. Your very first entry in your composition book will be "I want ..." Then put your first thought. Come up with a list of about twenty items. The next step is to prioritize your top 5 either by most essential or most immediate. Now we are going to refine the top five dreams. Starting with dream number one, ask yourself, "Why do I want this so much?"

We do this so we are focusing on the right dream. Let's say that your dream is to have ten million dollars. That is not your dream. Your dream is what that ten million dollars can get you. You can say that you could buy a fancy house and nice cars. Well, you're still not there yet. Now if you say something like I want a family with a spouse, 2.8 children, two wiener dogs, a cat, and a four-bedroom house, a pool area with a built-in barbeque, and an SUV to take the kids to soccer practice, you're on your dreams.

> *"People don't buy WHAT you do;*
> *they buy WHY you do it."*
> *~ Simon Sinek*

Why ask why? The "Why" is the greatest motivator. Tony Robbins says it is 70 times more important than how or what. It is the reason one gets out of bed every morning. Why is the reason we go to work or start a business? If you have children or a significant other, then you probably already know at least one reason why. Now let's find more reasons why. You may have to search deep into yourself and your dreams to find the answer.

For example, my dream is to write and publish this book. If you are reading this now, then I have accomplished my goal. Yay me! Now I ask myself "Why do I want to write this book?" The superficial reason one may think of is that I want to sell a lot of books and make some money. Well, there are millions of ways to make money. There are unlimited products, services, and investments I could do for the same goal. So, why do I want to write the book? I then would brainstorm with myself and search deeply. In my composition book, I write down possible reasons 'why' until I come up with one (or more). Here is what I came up with. Working with my students, I found a desire to help them succeed and it is partially for them, and others like them. I also want to leave a legacy for my children. Since my children are entering their teen years, they are currently not listening to anything I have to say about anything. So, when they're in their late twenties or early thirties, I hope they will read my book. Maybe then they will believe Daddy knew what he was talking about. I also want a legacy for the world and to be a part of history. It is my way of saying Jerry Coy was here, and he left this for you. That is a sweet little bonus if I make a few bucks selling books.

Now repeat the brainstorming reasons "why" for the top five dreams on your list. When you discover your real reasons why, then highlight them and this becomes your purpose. Now we need to make visual cues. Write out or print your dreams and your purpose and post them where you spend considerable time. You could also use a dry-erase marker and write them on your bathroom mirror. That way you have daily cues when you brush your teeth, shave, or put on makeup every morning. Another popular method is to create what is called a Vision Board. You can designate some wall space or go buy a pin-board. Search the internet for pictures that symbolize your dreams and post them on your vision board. For example, if you want a five-bedroom house with a three-car garage, find the right photo to print and pin it. If your dream is six-pack abs, print and pin a picture. Be sure to put this vision board in a conspicuous space within your home or workspace where you spend time looking at it. Update it frequently.

This is using a principle known as the Law of Attraction. This Law of Attraction is "like attracts like". When I first learned of this law, it was explained as some mystical force that grants wishes if you focus on it. I was not in the right mindset to accept this secret. After my journey of audiobooks and research, the Law of Attraction makes total sense now. You don't need Jedi powers to use this law. I prefer the neuroscience explanation, The Law of Attraction simply states that where attention goes, energy flows. Keeping the attention on your dreams and goals, you are more likely to achieve them. The vision board is one tool used to keep the attention where you need it. The visual cues keep you on task and visualization of the attainment of your dreams motivates you to keep working on what you want.

One of my students recorded in his composition book his dream of owning a Tesla Cybertruck. I suggested that he find the one he wants and print a photo for his vision board; better yet go to the dealership and have the salesman take a photo of him behind the wheel for the vision board. That way he can visualize himself owning it.

> *"Whatever The Mind Can Conceive and Believe, It Can Achieve"*
> *~Napoleon Hill*

Visualization is using a strong mental image of your life in the future after you achieve your goals. Also, imagine the feeling you will have. If you visualize success, you can feel the success and build the self-confidence you need. One of the earliest authors I know of who first wrote about this technique is Napoleon Hill in his book *"Think and Grow Rich*" in 1937. Napoleon interviewed and studied several highly successful people of his time to see if a common factor made them so rich and successful. He found a mindset that they all had in common. I will discuss Napoleon again in later chapters. Several highly successful people have attributed the Law of Attraction and visualization to their success. Oprah Winfrey, Steve Harvey, Ellen DeGeneres, and Beyonce have often discussed using vision boards. Will Smith is a huge fan of the Law of Attraction. Jim Carrey wrote himself a ten-million-dollar check and kept it with him until he could cash it. He was paid $10 Million for his role in *Dumb and Dumber*. Fitness dreams can also be fulfilled with visualization. Arnold Schwarzenegger speaks of the power of visualization.

Now that you have defined your dreams, you are on your way to achieving your goals. But first, we must set our goals. The principles we've already learned can set you apart from others who don't have these tools. Now we will go further to program your brain and motivate you to start on your dreams.

Activity for Step 1: Defining Your Dreams

Objective: Crystalizing your dreams, making them tangible, and setting the foundation for your actions. By physically articulating these dreams, we reinforce our commitment to them, giving them life beyond mere thought.

Materials Needed: Composition book, pen or pencil, access to a printer or magazines for visuals, and a quiet space for introspection.

1. **Deep Dive into Dreams:** Start by closing your eyes and taking a deep breath. Let your mind wander to your heart's desires without

judgment. Once you have a clear picture, open your eyes and in your composition book, list down these dreams, no matter how big or small.

2. **Discover the "Why" Behind Your Dreams:** For each dream listed, dive deep to discover why you want to achieve it. Write a paragraph for each dream detailing the "why" behind it. This will serve as a continuous source of motivation.

3. **Morning Mirror Motivation:** Select the top 5 dreams that resonate most with you from your list. Write these down on paper and post them on your bathroom mirror. This ensures that you're reminded of your aspirations every morning, helping you start your day with purpose.

4. **Craft Your Vision Board:** This activity is fun, hands-on. Using visuals from magazines or printed from the internet, create a vision board representing each of your dreams. For instance, if you dream of traveling to Paris, you might include an image of the Eiffel Tower. Place this board somewhere you'll see it daily, reinforcing your dreams continuously.

5. **Visualization and Emotion:** Dedicate a few minutes each day to sit quietly, looking at your vision board. Try to not only see but feel your dreams. If it's that house you want, imagine the warmth of the living room, the smell of your favorite meal being cooked, or the laughter of your family in the background. Emotionally connect with your dreams, making them more real than ever.

6. **Daily Reflection:** At the end of every day, reflect on your actions. How did they bring you closer to your dreams? Jot down these reflections in your composition book. This process will help you identify patterns and behaviors that work in your favor.

Remember, the power of putting pen to paper should never be underestimated. This activity is designed to make you dream and feel, live, and eventually achieve those dreams. The path to success begins with clarity of purpose, and these exercises are your first step towards that clarity.

Chapter 10
Step 2 - Set Your Goals

"The tragedy in life doesn't lie in not reaching your goal. The tragedy lies in having no goals to reach." ~Benjamin Mays

---

In Step 2 of this book's 7-step process, we diverge from the traditional S.M.A.R.T goals framework to introduce a version that better aligns with the journey to manifesting your dreams. While many versions of S.M.A.R.T goals emphasize attributes like 'Achievable,' the 'A' in our framework stands for 'Ambitious,' reflecting the need for goals that push you beyond your comfort zone. This modification is critical for setting the stage for your Massive Action Plan, effectively bridging the gap between your dreams and actionable milestones. This revised S.M.A.R.T framework—Specific, Measurable, Ambitious, Realistic, and Timely goals—provides a more robust foundation for making your dreams a reality.

"Dreams without goals, are just dreams and they ultimately fuel disappointment"
~Denzel Washington

Many have said that less than 3% of people set and write down their goals and less than 1% achieve these specific goals. These numbers have been made up but are probably accurate. However, according to the (Mathews, 2007) Study, conducted by Dr. Gail Matthews, focused on the effectiveness of writing down goals. "Group 2 achieved significantly more goals than Group 1". The difference between these groups is that Group 2 wrote down their goals. All the groups that wrote down their goals significantly achieved more than the group (1) that did not. Goals written down are 42% better than those not in writing. The study thus underscores the power of clearly defining, writing down, and regularly reviewing one's goals to increase the likelihood of achieving them.

Now that we have defined our dreams in Chapter 1, we must set our goals. There is a very important difference in how we word our dreams and our goals. You may have heard of the acronym for S.M.A.R.T. Goals. I have heard a few different versions. The following is my favorite. My version of SMART stands for Specific, Measurable, Ambitious, Realistic, and Timely. I will now break down these components.

Specific

Dreams often lack specificity and can be tenuous, such as wanting to "have an attractive physique." While these dreams provide a starting point and offer a sense of direction, they are usually too vague to act upon directly. On the other hand, goals serve as concrete milestones on the path to making your dreams a reality. A well-defined goal in this context would be to "achieve a body fat percentage of 18% while building muscle mass." Adding quantifiable metrics enables a way to measure and track your progress, making the journey toward your dream more actionable and aligned with the 7-step process laid out in this book.

Measurable

A crucial aspect of goal setting is incorporating measurable indicators to track your progress effectively. If you dream of having an "attractive physique," a measurable goal could involve targeting a specific body fat percentage and quantifying muscle mass gains. For example, you might aim to achieve a body fat percentage of 18% while increasing your muscle mass by 10 pounds. In financial contexts, specificity could mean setting a goal to earn an extra $20,000 this year. The key is to choose quantifiable metrics whenever possible to gauge your progress accurately.

You can establish qualitative but still specific indicators for goals that are harder to quantify, such as achieving a six-pack. In this case, you might aim for a "visible definition of all six abdominal muscles" as your criterion for success or a body-fat percentage of less than 10 percent. These measurable or qualitatively specific indicators align closely with the 7-step process in this book, particularly when you're crafting a Massive Action Plan that demands clear, achievable benchmarks.

Ambitious

"One never achieves greatness by staying in their comfort zone."
-Jerry Coy.

Goals should push you beyond the bounds of your comfort zone, and that's precisely why the 'A' in the S.M.A.R.T. framework, as described in this book, stands for 'Ambitious' rather than 'Achievable.' Setting easily attainable goals may provide quick wins but lack the transformative power to propel you significantly closer to your dreams. Ambitious goals act like catalysts, accelerating your journey and offering greater growth and fulfillment opportunities. Even if you fall short of meeting these lofty objectives, you will find yourself much further along the path to your dreams than those who either set easily achievable goals or have no goals. This approach aligns well with the 7-step process, especially when formulating your Massive Action Plan, where ambition drives your actions.

"Go big or go BIGGER"
~Grant Cardone

Realistic

I said to be ambitious but not unreasonable. "I want to lose 20 pounds by Friday" is not a realistic goal. As a personal trainer, I had a client who wanted to fit into her wedding dress that she bought 2 sizes too small. This bride-to-be would ask me to help her with that goal. "I said no problem. When is the wedding?" She would reply, "In just over a month." At that moment, I realized she was serious. It takes about six weeks to lose one dress size the healthy way.

You will need to find a good balance between ambitious and realistic. If your goal is too ambitious, you may find yourself taking shortcuts. In the bride example above, the bride may encourage herself to take unhealthy measures to lose weight, leading to eating disorders or worse. The salesman who sets goals too high may find themself conducting business in a less than ethical manner to meet an unrealistic goal. These practices may cause someone to lose licensing, customers, or jobs.

A realistic relationship goal would be to get married by the end of the year only if you are currently dating someone. Many women I see on social media say they will only date a man over 6'2" who earns at least $250,000 a year and of course, the six-pack abs. Let's break it down.

Quantifying the odds of the "average woman" finding and marrying a man who meets all these criteria is challenging. It would require a comprehensive analysis of numerous variables including geographical location, social factors, and personal preferences, among others. However, we can make some general observations suggesting the odds are quite low.

Height: About 14.5% of adult men in the United States are 6'2" or taller, according to the Centers for Disease Control and Prevention (CDC). The percentage may vary in other countries.

Income: According to the U.S. Census Bureau, only a small percentage of individuals earn $250,000 or more per year. In 2019, approximately 9% of households (which often include more than one income earner) had an income of $200,000 or more.

Physical Fitness: The percentage of men with "six-pack abs" is hard to quantify, but it's safe to assume that it's a small minority, given that achieving and maintaining that level of physical fitness requires a significant commitment to diet and exercise.

Single and Interested in Marriage: Additionally, not all men who meet these criteria will be single or interested in marriage.

Compatibility: Beyond these criteria, there's also the matter of mutual compatibility, shared life goals, emotional connection, and other factors that are crucial to a successful marriage.

When you combine all these factors, it's evident that the subset of men who meet all these criteria is exceedingly small. Therefore, the odds for an "average woman" to find and marry such a man would likely be extremely low.

That said, it's worth noting that while these attributes (height, income, physical fitness) are specific and quantifiable, they don't necessarily predict marital happiness or success. A successful and fulfilling marriage is often built on less tangible factors like mutual respect, communication, and shared values.

For guys who have a goal of marrying Jessica Alba, well that is of course extremely unrealistic. Jessica is a wealthy celebrity who is already married with children and way too busy to meet you. Let's revise that goal. Based on the underlying dream, one can set more realistic and achievable goals. For example, if the dream reflects a desire for a strong, passionate relationship, the goal could be to date more actively and seek partners who are genuinely compatible in terms of values, interests, and mutual attraction.

Remember that a meaningful relationship is built on more than external characteristics like looks or fame. If you're focused on superficial attributes, you might miss the chance to find someone genuinely compatible. The goal should not be to marry someone who ticks off certain boxes but to build a happy, fulfilling life that might include a meaningful relationship as one component.

Timely

Setting a time frame for achieving your goals is a crucial element in effective goal setting, which is why the 'T' in the S.M.A.R.T framework outlined in this book stands for 'Timely.' Without a defined timeline, goals can become elusive, perpetually deferred dreams. For instance, if you aspire to land your dream job, you might first need to graduate, earn a certification, and obtain a license. Estimate the duration of these prerequisites and set a deadline that accounts for them. On the other hand, some goals like quitting smoking don't require a long-term timeline; the ideal time to start is right now. Incorporating a time frame is particularly valuable when crafting your Massive Action Plan, ensuring you're marking milestones and progressing toward them promptly.

Writing down your goals and sub-goals (milestones)

Goals must be written down or you cannot take yourself seriously. For each dream, you must have at least one goal written down. Some dreams may take stages of goals before your dream is reached. For example, you may have a goal of 1 million dollars in one year. That sounds unrealistic but it is not. You will probably need some smaller "sub-goals" to help you get the main goal. "I will need to make fifty sales by the end of each month" would be a sub-goal. You can also break it down into more sub-goals;" I will need to call one hundred people a day to make fifty sales by the end of each month." These numbers may of course vary depending on your product or industry.

Having these goals written down at your workstation can help you stay on task. There is a special way to phrase the goals that can help you visualize success. Goals must be expressed as already achieved. "I have $1 Million by the end of next year." or "I do make one hundred cold calls today and every day." Which do you think is more powerful: ``I am trying to quit smoking" or "I am a non-smoker!"? The latter is of course way more powerful, and your subconscious brain will respond to it better. Remember, a goal does not become official until it is written down.

Reaffirm your goals daily. Write them down on your bathroom mirror with a dry-erase marker. Verbally recite them aloud as you shave or put on makeup.

David Goggins, author, and endurance athlete, calls it the accountability mirror. He talks to himself in the mirror because that is the one person you cannot lie to. That person in the mirror is the only person to blame if things go wrong and the only person who you can count

Jerry Coy

on to fix it. Tell that person in the mirror what you want to accomplish today and your long-term goals.

When revising your plans, only revise to make them more specific, measurable, ambitious, more... you get the idea, more S.M.A.R.T. Don't revise your goals because you gave up on them. If your goal aligns with your dreams, don't give up on them unless you realize it is unrealistic.

Note About Fitness Goals

An important note about fitness goals is an effective measure of your progress. Only use the bathroom scale to measure your goals if you are on the wrestling or boxing team and must be within a specific fighting class. The bathroom scale is a horrible way to measure your fitness level. Fitness goals should be performance-based. For example, your goal could be to run a certain distance within a particular time, lift a specific amount of weight in a bench press, etc. Suppose your goal is to lose weight; instead of the bathroom scale, which is a wildly inaccurate way to measure your progress, use a measuring tape around your waist or pants size as a goal. Remember to measure and record your milestones along the way. Don't do weekly weigh-ins since we are not using weight as a goal.

Measuring this fitness goal would involve tracking your run times and distances. You could use a running app or a simple stopwatch to monitor your pace and total time. Each week, you'd aim to see improvement—either running the same distance faster or finding that you can run longer without feeling fatigued.

In this example, the weight on the bathroom scale becomes irrelevant. What matters is your performance: Can you run a 5K faster than when you started? Do you feel more robust and more enduring? These performance-based metrics align well with the approach laid out in this book, particularly in Step 2, "Set Your Goals," and Step 3, "Massive Action Plan," providing an actionable, measurable pathway to achieving your more significant dreams.

A daily goal I often like to use involves my Apple Watch. You're probably unfamiliar with the three rings if you don't have one. These rings represent the standing, activity, and exercise goals. I often tell myself I'm not allowed to watch television until all three goal rings are closed. If you don't want to use the watch, tell yourself no television until you've spent an hour of exercise at the gym.

Activity for Step 2:
Setting Goals and Writing Them Down

Specific, Measurable, Ambitious, Realistic, and Timely. Remember to be precise and aim for quantifiable metrics, pushing yourself out of your comfort zone while keeping them within the realms of possibility. Complete the following for each of the top 5 dreams from step 1.

Write Them Down Officially: Choose a page in your journal, notebook, or whiteboard to be your "Official Goals" page. Write down these 3-5 S.M.A.R.T goals, using powerful affirmations like "I have achieved X by [specific date]." Make sure they are in a place you can revisit often.

Jerry Coy

Sub-Goals (Milestones): Identify 1-3 sub-goals or milestones for each of your top goals to help you achieve the larger goal. For example, if your main goal is to save $12,000 by the end of the year, a milestone might be to save $1,000 each month.

Visualization: Take a moment to close your eyes and visualize achieving each goal. How does it feel? What does it look like? Try to involve all your senses.

Affirmations: Create a daily affirmation for each goal. These should be positive, present-tense statements like, "I am confidently working towards achieving X." or "Every day, I am closer to Y."

Daily Reminder: Write down your goals on sticky notes, index cards, or in a digital reminder. Place them around your home or workspace or set them as reminders on your phone. This will serve as a daily cue to keep your goals in mind.

Review and Adjust: At the end of each week, take 10-15 minutes to review your goals. Celebrate your progress, even if small, and adjust your approach if needed. This is essential for maintaining momentum and ensuring you're on the right track.

Share Your Goals: If comfortable, share your goals with a friend or family member who can offer encouragement and accountability.

Reflection:
1. How did you feel while setting your S.M.A.R.T. goals? Were you excited, overwhelmed, motivated?

2. What potential challenges do you foresee in achieving these goals? How can you prepare for or overcome them?

3. How will achieving these goals bring you closer to your dream?

Commitment:

Write a commitment statement in your journal or notebook at the end of your activity. "I, [Your Name], commit to passionately pursuing these goals and taking consistent action towards achieving my dream of [Your Dream]. I understand that there will be challenges, but I am prepared to face them with determination and resilience."

Seal it with a signature and date to mark your commitment.

Remember, writing down your goals and revisiting them regularly is a powerful tool in manifesting your dreams. Stay consistent, be patient with yourself, and celebrate every win, no matter how small.

Chapter 11
Step 3 - Massive Action Plan

"Action is the foundational key to all success."
~Pablo Picasso

An action plan serves as the strategic and tactical blueprint for achieving your goals, effectively addressing the "How" after you've established the " why " in Step 1 and 'what" in Step 2: "Set Your Goals." In the context of this 7-step framework in "Start on Your Dreams," an action plan involves outlining specific tasks, timelines, resources, and milestones. It's essentially a detailed road map that clearly states what needs to be done, when it needs to be done, and how you intend to do it. Developing a robust action plan creates a systematic pathway to convert your ambitious goals into actionable steps, making achieving your dreams more manageable and less overwhelming.

A well-crafted action plan comprises multiple layers, breaking down large tasks into smaller, more manageable tasks. Each task is associated with a specific timeline for completion and may include additional information like required resources, potential obstacles, and criteria for success. By segmenting large tasks into smaller ones and associating deadlines with each, you build a sense of urgency, accountability, and trackability into your goal-achieving process. This also enables you to monitor progress effectively and adjust as needed, aligning with Step 6: "Fail and Pivot" and Step 7: "Execute Revised Plan" of this framework.

For example, let's say your goal is to write and publish a novel within two years, a goal set in Step 2 of this book's framework. Your action plan might involve tasks like researching your book's genre, outlining the story, setting aside dedicated writing hours each week, and identifying publishing options. Each of these tasks could be further broken down: for instance, "conducting research" could involve reading three top books in your genre and completing this within a month. "Outlining the story" could be a week-long task involving brainstorming sessions and refining the structure. With a comprehensive action plan, you're not just stating that you want to write a novel—you're specifying how you'll achieve each component of that broader goal.

Grant Cardone, a renowned entrepreneur and motivational speaker, popularized "Taking Massive Action" to achieve extraordinary results in business and personal life. According to Cardone, taking regular or moderate action is insufficient for realizing ambitious goals or dreams; one must go above and beyond, exerting extraordinary effort and commitment to break through barriers and achieve success. He argues that most people underestimate the work and persistence required to reach their goals, leading to disappointment and failure. In contrast, taking "Massive Action" means multiplying your efforts, pushing boundaries, and doing whatever it takes to overcome obstacles and achieve your objectives. This approach aligns well with

Step 3: "Massive Action Plan" within this book, emphasizing that a robust and committed approach is essential for turning goals into reality.

"Never lower your target; increase your actions."
~Grant Cardone

NO PLAN B! This reflects an all-in commitment to your primary goal or dream. It's based on the idea that having a fallback plan can subtly undermine your efforts to achieve your primary objective by providing an easier, less challenging alternative when obstacles arise. In the context of the 7-step framework in "Start on Your Dreams," if your action plan in Step 3 truly aligns with your dream established in Step 1, then having a Plan B could serve as a distraction or even a mental safety net, which could decrease your urgency and resolve. By eliminating the option of a Plan B, you intensify your focus and efforts toward your primary goal, thereby harnessing all your energy, resources, and time in one direction. This doesn't mean you don't adapt or pivot when challenges occur—those are covered in Step 6: "Fail and Pivot" and Step 7: "Execute Revised Plan." But these pivots are adjustments within the framework of achieving your original dream, not shifts to an entirely different goal or dream.

"If you talk about it, it's a dream;
if you envision it, it's possible, but if you
schedule it, it's real."
~Tony Robbins

Tony Robbins' Rapid Planning Method (RPM) is a time-management and productivity system designed to help individuals focus not just on tasks but also on the results they want to achieve and why those results are essential. The RPM system emphasizes the significance of knowing your "Why" or the ultimate purpose behind your actions, as this provides the emotional fuel to drive you forward. Then, the method encourages you to be crystal-clear about the "What" or the specific results you aim to accomplish. Finally, the "How" comes into play, detailing the steps or tasks required to achieve those results. In essence, RPM is a holistic approach to planning that combines the motivational power of having a clear purpose (the "Why") with actionable, results-focused steps (the "What" and "How"), aligning well with the early stages of your 7-step process in "Start on Your Dreams."

Write down your action plan in your journal. When drafting the plan, you must have clear objectives based on goals from step 2. Have your goals written down in a visible area like your bathroom mirror or on a poster board in your home office. Review and revise your goals every day. Since your goals from step 2 are measurable, measure your progress regularly,

Fitness Plans

Making your fitness goals performance-based necessitates a more structured and nuanced action plan, perfectly aligning with Step 3: "Massive Action Plan" in this book. Instead of merely visiting the gym five days a week, consider crafting a detailed weekly regimen targeting various fitness components to enhance your overall performance. Each gym session could have specific objectives directly correlating to your broader performance-based goals.

For example, Mondays and Thursdays could be devoted to cardiovascular improvement, to complete at least 30 minutes of high-intensity interval training (HIIT) to boost your running speed and endurance. On Tuesdays and Fridays, the focus could shift to strength training involving targeted resistance exercises like squats, lunges, and deadlifts. Aim to complete at least four sets of each, and within each set, have a defined rep range and weight level to build muscle strength progressively. On Wednesdays, you could engage in activities that improve your flexibility and core strength, incorporating yoga and focused core exercises to enhance balance and reduce the risk of injury. Of course, your fitness plan would vary depending on your specific goals: consult your trainer (see step 4).

Keep a workout log or use a fitness tracking app to ensure that you're making measurable progress. Document the time you take for your HIIT sessions, the amount of weight you lift during resistance training, and any improvements in your flexibility and core strength routines. This meticulous record-keeping allows you to assess your performance over time and tweak your action plan as needed, which fits seamlessly with the principles of Step 6: "Fail and Pivot" and Step 7: "Execute Revised Plan" in this book.

By adopting this approach, you develop a comprehensive, performance-based fitness action plan that doesn't just fulfill time quotas but actively works towards achieving your overarching dream.

Activity for Step 3: Drafting a Massive Action Plan

Materials Needed:

- A journal or notebook (Alternatively, you could use a whiteboard, digital document, or a project management tool like Trello)
- A pen or marker
- Optional: A calendar or scheduling tool

Instructions:

Brainstorm Tasks: Start by jotting down every task that comes to mind which you think needs to be done to achieve your goal. Be as specific as possible. For instance, if your goal is to open a coffee shop, tasks might include "research location," "develop a business plan," "source suppliers," etc.

Prioritize: Not all tasks are created equal. Rank the tasks in order of importance and urgency. Determine which tasks are foundational and must be done before others.

Break It Down: Subdivide larger, more complex tasks into smaller, manageable parts. For example, "develop a business plan" can be broken down into "conduct market research," "calculate budget," "outline marketing strategy," and so on.

Assign Deadlines: Attach a realistic yet ambitious, deadline to each task. Use a calendar to visualize when each task needs to be completed.

Assign Ownership: If you've already assembled your team from Step 4, assign specific tasks to specific team members based on their skills and roles.

Sequence Tasks: Identify any dependencies between tasks and order them logically. For example, you can't "sign a lease" before you "research and choose a location."

Review: Once you've drafted your plan, take a moment to review it for coherence and feasibility. Adjust as needed.

Commit To Action: Write down the first task you'll complete and set a reminder in your phone or calendar. This is your immediate following action.

Reflection:

After completing this activity, you'll have a detailed Massive Action Plan with tasks, deadlines, and assigned responsibilities. This plan is your roadmap, and while it may need adjustments along the way, it gives you a clear path toward achieving your dreams. By planning and breaking your goal down into actionable steps, you're dramatically increasing your odds of success.

Keep this plan accessible and review it regularly. It's a living document that will evolve as you progress, face challenges, and learn more about achieving your goals.

Additional Massive Action Plan Activity for Step 3

This activity aims to provide readers with a concrete method to take their broad goals from Step 2 and convert them into specific, actionable tasks. This action plan provides a roadmap for the journey ahead, offering clarity and direction.

Dreams are ethereal, distant, and often intangible. Yet, when dreams are coupled with a Massive Action Plan, they begin their transformation into reality. The goal of this activity is not just to have a dream but to create a clear pathway that makes its realization possible. Remember, action is necessary for the best intentions in the world to help you achieve your dreams.

Activity: Crafting Your Massive Action Plan

1. **Brainstorm Tasks**:

Open your journal and list every task related to your dream. Think granular. If you dream of publishing a book, don't just write "write a book." Instead, jot down specific tasks like "outline chapters," "create a writing schedule," or "find a literary agent."

2. **Prioritize**:

Every dream has essential pillars. What are the non-negotiable tasks without which your dream cannot stand? Rank these tasks in terms of their importance.

3. **Break It Down**:

Jerry Coy

Now, refine your tasks. For each primary task, what are the smaller sub-tasks? For instance, if one of your tasks was to "develop a marketing plan," break it down into "identify target audience," "choose marketing channels," and "allocate budget."

4. Set Deadlines:

Without a timeline, a plan is just a wish. Assign a deadline to each task and sub-task. When do you aim to complete it? This creates urgency and a sense of commitment.

5. Assign Ownership:

If you're working with a team, delegate tasks. Who is best equipped to handle each task? Remember, collaboration can make the journey smoother and more efficient.

6. Sequence Tasks:

Specific tasks depend on others. Map out a sequence. What must be done first, second, third, and so on?

7. Review and Revise:

Your initial plan might not be perfect, and that's okay. Review it, spot the gaps, and revise. You may have forgotten a crucial task, or some tasks are more significant than initially thought. Adjust accordingly.

8. Commit:

Identify the first task on your list – the immediate action you must take. When will you start? Commit. Set a date and time for tomorrow morning or following Monday.

Reflection and Next Steps:

With your Massive Action Plan, you're no longer just dreaming but on a defined path toward realization. This plan should be a living entity, evolving as you progress, learn, and grow. Stick to it, but also allow yourself the flexibility to adapt when needed.

End each week by reviewing your plan. Celebrate the tasks you've accomplished and strategize for the upcoming ones. Stay accountable. Remember, it's not about perfection but progression.

No matter how vast, every dream can be broken down into actionable tasks. You're setting the stage for success with persistence, clarity, and a well-thought-out Massive Action Plan.

"A goal without a plan is just a wish." Today, you've turned your wish into a plan. Now, it's time to act."
~Antoine de Saint-Exupéry

Chapter 12
Step 4 - Assemble Your Team

"If you want to go fast, go alone.
If you want to go far, go together."
– African Proverb

Following the 'why,' the 'who' holds the next level of importance. While understanding our motivations and reasons provides a foundational drive, recognizing the right people to be involved in our journey becomes equally crucial. Surrounding ourselves with those who share our vision, support our aspirations, and complement our strengths can be the difference between mere dreams and tangible success.

The concept of the Mastermind involves a harmonious gathering of two or more individuals who come together to solve problems or achieve goals. In this setting, each person's intellect, experience, and skills complement those of the others, creating a more potent collective intelligence than any individual could achieve alone. This concept fits seamlessly into Step 4 of this book's 7-step process, which involves assembling your team to provide diverse perspectives and skill sets.

Napoleon Hill, who popularized the Mastermind principle in his book "Think and Grow Rich," argued that a Mastermind group could provide a "third mind"—a synergistic effect where the collective intelligence surpasses the sum of the group's intellects. According to Hill, a Mastermind group offers moral and mental support, provides diverse skills and perspectives, and holds each member accountable to their goals. This is essential for anyone striving to transform their dreams into reality, as the collective problem-solving and accountability aspects of a Mastermind group can dramatically accelerate progress toward achieving ambitious objectives.

"No two minds ever come together without creating a third, invisible, intangible force, which may be likened to a third mind [the master mind]." ~Napoleon Hill

---

It's a common misconception that successful individuals achieve their dreams solely through their efforts. Virtually all high-achieving people had help along the way. Whether it's mentors who offer invaluable insights, teams who execute the vision, or even critics who provide constructive feedback, the role of external influences cannot be overstated. This underscores the importance of Step 4 in the 7-step process outlined in this book, which advocates assembling a team. By bringing together a group of capable, like-minded individuals, you're adding the workforce and multiplying the intellectual resources and skills at your disposal.

Take the examples of some of the world's billionaires to illustrate this point. Jeff Bezos, the founder of Amazon, didn't build his retail empire alone; he had an army of engineers, strategists, and leaders who helped realize his vision. Similarly, Elon Musk oversees multiple ventures like SpaceX, Tesla, and Neuralink, each with specialized teams working to advance humanity in various ways. Even Warren Buffett, often heralded for his investment acumen, frequently attributes his success to his partnership with Charlie Munger and his team at Berkshire Hathaway. These examples demonstrate that having a solid team is beneficial and often essential to achieving lofty ambitions.

Contrary to popular belief, assembling a team can mean something other than hiring a full-fledged staff of employees. There are various cost-effective ways to build a support system to help you achieve your dreams, as this book outlines in Step 4 of the 7-step process. One invaluable but often underutilized resource is mentorship. A mentor can provide expertise, guidance, and feedback to accelerate your progress toward your goals dramatically. The best part? Many mentors offer their time and knowledge for free to give back and invest in the next generation.

Outsourcing is another practical option, especially for specific tasks that don't require a permanent team member. Websites like Fiverr, Upwork, or TaskRabbit offer a plethora of freelancers skilled in everything from graphic design to coding to marketing. Virtual assistants can also be hired to manage routine tasks, freeing you to focus on higher-value activities only you can do. This aligns well with Step 3, which emphasizes creating a Massive Action Plan to streamline your path to success.

So, even if you're working on a tight budget, don't let the lack of a traditional "team" deter you. With some creativity and resourcefulness, you can assemble a group of mentors, freelancers, and virtual assistants to provide the support, skills, and accountability you need to make your dreams a reality.

Real estate investing is a prime example of an endeavor that calls for a diversified team, reinforcing the significance of Step 4 in the 7-step process described in this book. If you aim to become a successful real estate investor or landlord, you'll quickly realize it's a more than one-person show. Each team member plays a critical role in your investment journey and brings a unique set of skills that you, as an individual, may not possess.

Firstly, you'll need a real estate agent who understands investment properties and can help you find properties that match your criteria. An agent can negotiate deals on your behalf, leveraging their market knowledge to get you the best price. Then comes the inspector, who is crucial in assessing the property's condition to prevent unforeseen costs later. A financial broker can assist you in securing the necessary capital or mortgage at the most favorable terms, helping to maximize your investment returns. And let's remember contractors; these professionals will renovate or maintain your property, impacting both its value and desirability to tenants.

Each of these experts contributes to a different aspect of real estate investing, and their coordinated efforts can help you avoid pitfalls and succeed in a highly competitive market. By thoughtfully assembling this team, you are essentially enacting your Massive Action Plan from Step 3, but with the added advantage of specialized knowledge from various fields. This synergistic approach significantly enhances your chances of achieving your real estate investment goals.

When running my physiotherapy practice, I fell into the trap of becoming a jack-of-all-trades, handling everything from website development to appointment scheduling, marketing, and even laundry. Looking back, I can't help but wonder how much more successful my practice could have been if I'd enlisted help to take on some of those tasks. Delegating would have freed up my time to focus on the core activities that could elevate my business, effectively implementing Step 4 of the 7-step process in this book.

The same principle applies to my podcast, where I outsource the recording of the intro and outro segments. While I could have spent weeks figuring out the best way to produce these segments, a skilled professional from Fiverr was able to complete them overnight. This expedited the process, saved me valuable time, and likely resulted in a higher-quality product. Whether you're a solopreneur or running a more extensive operation, strategically outsourcing tasks can provide a significant advantage, enabling you to move closer to your goals more efficiently.

While some coaches advocate for keeping your goals and plans close to the vest to avoid external negativity, I propose an alternative approach: finding an "accountability partner." Having someone you trust to keep you focused can be invaluable, as a real-world manifestation of Step 4 in the 7-step process detailed in this book. This person or group can remind you of your commitments, challenge you when you're slacking, and celebrate your wins, creating a positive feedback loop that fuels your motivation.

For example, I once enlisted my students as accountability partners to help lower my resting heart rate. Making my goal public within a supportive community adds a layer of encouraging and practical accountability. The collective effort helped me stay committed, and knowing that I would have to report back on my progress instilled a sense of urgency and focus that I might not have had otherwise. In short, the right kind of accountability can be a powerful catalyst in your journey to achieve your goals.

Involving your spouse and family in setting and achieving your goals can be incredibly beneficial. These people often know you best and have a vested interest in your success, making them ideal partners for brainstorming, planning, and serving as sounding boards. Incorporating them into various stages of your 7-step process can help you see angles you might not have considered, fine-tune your action plans, and provide emotional support when the going gets tough. They can serve as indispensable team members in Step 4 of the process outlined in this book, offering a variety of perspectives that could enhance your plans and make your dreams more attainable.

Moreover, looping in your family and spouse creates a collective investment in your journey, which can be both motivating and rewarding. Sharing your dreams and plans with them makes you more accountable and nurtures a shared vision of success that can strengthen familial bonds. The conversations you have while brainstorming or problem-solving can also serve as educational moments for younger family members, imparting the importance of goal-setting and strategic planning. Thus, the benefits of involving your loved ones in your quest extend beyond the immediate goal, fostering a culture of aspiration and achievement within your family unit.

Jerry Coy

I am currently involving my wife and our friends to proofread this book. At first, my wife said she didn't have the time to read it for me until I told her there was a section about her. When she asked me what I wrote about her, I told her she would have to read it to find out. I, of course, only told her to get her to read it for me. So, this is the section about her in my book. Honey, if you're reading this now, there's more about you in the later chapters; keep reading.

Incorporating fitness and nutrition professionals into your Massive Action Plan (Step 3) is a game-changing strategy to make your fitness dreams a reality. Studies suggest that individuals who work with personal trainers often experience more significant improvements in strength and other fitness metrics than those who go it alone. For example, research published in the Journal of Sports Science & Medicine has found that working with a personal trainer can lead to better outcomes in achieving fitness goals. These professionals can provide specific, targeted exercises and routines tailored to your body's needs, offering a measurable and timely approach that aligns perfectly with Step 2: Set Your Goals.

Similarly, enlisting the aid of a registered dietitian or nutritionist can be equally transformative. A review article in the Journal of the Academy of Nutrition and Dietetics indicates that individualized medical nutrition therapy can enhance health outcomes significantly. When you make these experts part of your team in Step 4: Assemble Your Team, you're arming yourself with the knowledge and expertise that can vastly improve your chances of fitness success. Their specialized advice can serve as pivotal components of your overall plan, ensuring that every aspect of your fitness journey is optimized for the best results.

In Step 4, Assemble Your Team, you're doing more than just gathering people around you; you're strategically selecting experts, confidants, and accountability partners who will propel you toward your dreams and goals. This is not just about delegation; it's about leveraging collective wisdom, skill, and motivation. In doing so, you free yourself to focus on the core tasks only you can accomplish, multiplying your effectiveness and shortening the journey to your dream. A well-assembled team is not a luxury but a necessity, serving as the bedrock upon which the successful execution of your Massive Action Plan is built. By understanding each member's value and fostering a harmonious, mutually beneficial relationship with them, you're setting up a robust system geared for success. So, don't overlook this step; embrace it and use it as the fuel to drive you closer to making your dreams come true.

In achieving one's dreams, guidance from those who have trodden the path before can be invaluable. This is where a mentor comes into play. A mentor has accumulated wisdom, experience, and insights over the years and is willing to share these lessons with those coming up behind them. The relationship between a mentor and a mentee is one of guidance, support, and mutual respect, where knowledge and experiences are shared freely, aiding in the personal and professional growth of the mentee.

One of the standout advantages of having an experienced mentor is accelerating progress. Mentors can offer shortcuts, advice on avoiding common pitfalls, and insights on proven effective strategies. Essentially, they provide a roadmap that can save years of trial and error. Their hindsight becomes your foresight. Furthermore, they can provide access to networks and opportunities that might have taken much longer to come by independently.

111

While mentors' knowledge and strategic input are undoubtedly beneficial, their influence in shaping personal and professional skills can be even more profound. Through constructive feedback, they can help refine skills, enhance strengths, and address weaknesses. Their experiences serve as cautionary tales and inspirational stories, assisting mentees to build resilience, determination, and a growth mindset.

Beyond the professional realm, mentors often become a significant emotional and psychological support system. Achieving goals is as much an emotional journey as a practical one. There will be highs and lows, moments of doubt, and times of immense satisfaction. In these moments, having someone to share these feelings with, someone who genuinely understands and empathizes can be comforting and motivating. They become cheerleaders in success and pillars of strength in challenges, continually pushing their mentees toward their potential.

Lastly, mentorship isn't just about taking; it's also about giving back. Many mentors often express how the act of mentoring enriches their own lives. They see their knowledge and experiences shape another person's journey, which can be immensely rewarding. Once mentees achieve their goals, they're often inspired to become mentors themselves, passing on the legacy of knowledge and creating a cycle of continual growth and support.

While one can undoubtedly achieve success alone, having a mentor can make the journey smoother, faster, and more fulfilling. They don't just guide in the how-to but also instill confidence, nurture growth, and stand as shining examples of what's possible.

The company we keep profoundly shapes our aspirations, behaviors, and eventual outcomes in life. Whether we recognize it or not, our friends significantly influence our mindsets, attitudes, and actions. It's often said that we are the average of the five people we spend the most time with, underscoring the importance of surrounding ourselves with individuals who resonate with our dreams and aspirations.

When striving for success or a particular goal, it's vital to surround oneself with people who have either achieved your goal or are actively working towards similar ambitions. Their experiences, mindset, work ethic, and resilience can inspire and motivate. They understand the struggles, challenges, and sacrifices required to reach those pinnacles and can provide invaluable advice and guidance. Furthermore, witnessing their dedication and success is a tangible reminder that your goals are attainable, pushing you to persist.

Conversely, being around naysayers or those who don't share or understand your ambitions can be detrimental. They might unintentionally sow seeds of doubt, discourage risk-taking, or advocate for settling for mediocrity. Their perspectives, borne out of their fears and limitations, can become limiting beliefs for you if you're not mindful. It's not about severing ties but recognizing the influence and discerning the energy you allow into your space.

Additionally, a circle of driven individuals creates a positive feedback loop of aspiration and achievement. Celebrating each other's successes, learning from each other's failures, and consistently challenging one another to elevate can lead to exponential personal and collective growth. There's an inherent power in collective ambition. When one succeeds, it lifts the entire group, creating a culture of continuous progression.

Jerry Coy

While every individual in our life has unique value and significance, when it comes to realizing our dreams and ambitions, the influence of our immediate circle can't be overlooked. To reach the heights we desire, we must ensure that our process is filled with those who reflect where we want to be, not where we used to be. Such alignment accelerates our journey and makes it far more enriching and fulfilling.

Activity for Step 4: Assembling Your Team

Materials Needed:

- A journal or notebook (Whiteboard)
- A pen or marker
- Optional: Your phone or computer for research

Instructions:

1. **Identify Team Roles:** Reflect on your goals and consider what roles or expertise you need to achieve them. For example, if you want to start a coffee shop, you might need a real estate advisor, an accountant, a coffee supplier, etc.

2. **List Potential Team Members:** Write down the names of people you know who could fill these roles. They could be friends, family members, professionals, or mentors. If you don't know anyone suitable, jot down the kind of people you need to find.

3. **Reach Out**: Contact at least one person from your list to discuss your goals and see if they would be interested in being part of your team. You can wait to formalize something; the idea is to start the conversation.

4. **Research and Resources:** If there are roles you can't fill through your existing network, research online platforms, communities, or services where you can find the help you need. Websites like LinkedIn, Fiverr, and local business directories can be good starting points.

5. **Commitment Levels**: Only some team members need to be equally involved. Some might be advisors you consult occasionally, while others might work closely with you daily. Specify the level of commitment you expect from each team member.

6. **Record in Journal**: Write each team member's names, roles, and commitment levels in your journal or digital document. This will serve as your go-to reference as you move forward.

7. **First Team Meeting**: Schedule a meeting (virtual or in-person) with your assembled team to discuss the vision, the goals, and the roadmap. This is also an excellent time to discuss how you'll communicate and how often you'll meet moving forward.

Reflection:

After completing this activity, you should have a clearer picture of who is on your team and their role in helping you achieve your goals. This team will be instrumental as you face challenges and celebrate victories, providing practical assistance and emotional support.

Remember, Rome wasn't built in a day, nor did one person build it. Your team is your foundation, and you're setting yourself up for success by investing time in building strong relationships with team members.

Chapter 13
Step 5 - Execute Plan

"Ideas are easy. Implementation is hard."
~Guy Kawasaki

In Step 5: Execute Plan, the rubber meets the road. You've done the legwork: defined your dreams, set measurable and ambitious goals, created a Massive Action Plan, and assembled a formidable team. Now, it's time for action. There's a common temptation to delay starting, to say, "I'll begin on Monday," or "My New Year's resolution will finally start." But the power of now cannot be overstated. Step 5 is the 'when', and it is now. The perfect moment you're waiting for doesn't exist; the ideal moment is the one you decide to act in.

"I believe in resolutions; I just don't believe in waiting until the New Year."
~Jerry Coy

Delaying the start of your plan is often a form of procrastination or fear masquerading as prudence. The truth is, you're ready. You've followed the process and prepared yourself for this very moment. Putting it off until some arbitrary future date doesn't make your dreams more attainable; it makes them more distant. Starting right now is the key to bringing your dreams into reality. It's time to execute your plan; the best time to start is always now.

"The best time to plant a tree was 20 years ago. The second-best time is now."
~Chinese Proverb

In Grant Cardone's "The 10X Rule," the "Massive Action" concept is championed as the level of effort and commitment needed to achieve exceptional results. Cardone argues that most people underestimate the work required to meet their goals, leading to disappointment and failure. According to him, you need to aim ten times higher than you initially thought necessary and be prepared to do ten times more work. This 10X approach serves as a mental and operational framework that forces you to rethink everything regarding exponential growth, breaking you out of your comfort zone and propelling you toward unparalleled success. In executing your plan in Step 5, adopting the 10X mindset could be transformative, pushing you to maximize your efforts and accelerate your journey toward realizing your dreams.

"Massive action is the cure-all."
~Grant Cardone

In Step 5 of this book's 7-step process, "Execute Plan," the focus is on taking relentless action, which is perfectly echoed in the philosophy of motivational speaker Eric Thomas. One of Thomas's most iconic quotes says, "When you want to succeed as bad as you want to breathe, then you'll be successful." This statement is not just about the want or need to achieve; it's about the urgency and intensity with which you approach your objectives. When you treat your goals with the same non-negotiable necessity as breathing, failure is not an option.

Eric Thomas, popularly known as ET, has a motivational series called "Thank God It's Monday" (TGIM). The essence of TGIM is to flip the script on the typical dread associated with Mondays. For many people, Mondays signify the end of the weekend and the beginning of another grueling workweek. However, ET views Mondays as a fresh start, an opportunity to set the tone for the week and get ahead of the competition. His message is clear: if you start your week with enthusiasm and focus on your goals, you set yourself on a path to meet and exceed your expectations. By reframing Mondays as a day of opportunity rather than a day of dread, you align more closely with the relentless action and urgency Step 5 of this book encourages.

"When you want to succeed as bad as you want to breathe, then you'll be successful."
~Eric Thomas, aka ET the Hip Hop Preacher

Building on Thomas's concept of an unyielding drive, Step 5 encourages you to approach the execution of your plan with an uncompromising sense of dedication. It's about not merely going through the motions but immersing yourself wholeheartedly. When you execute your project with an intensity comparable to your need for air, the quality of your efforts elevates, boosting your likelihood of fulfilling your dreams. This level of commitment ensures that your execution phase is not a mere checkbox but a dynamic, evolving stage in your journey to manifest your dreams.

Executing a Massive Action Plan is not just about acting; it's about taking the right action. It's a concerted, relentless effort that aligns with your goals and dreams outlined in Steps 1 and 2 of this book. This isn't the time for half-measures or lukewarm commitments. Instead, a Massive Action Plan demands a total immersion into the tasks at hand, pushing past comfort zones and embracing risks. It's about proactively identifying roadblocks and creatively strategizing ways to overcome them.

Consistency is another crucial element when executing your Massive Action Plan. Taking massive action is not a one-off event but a continuous process. Step 5 is not just about initiating the plan but also

Jerry Coy

about sustaining momentum. Keep evaluating and re-evaluating your strategies, fine-tuning them as you learn from your successes and failures. Remember, an action plan is not set in stone; it's a dynamic blueprint that will likely need adjustments along the way, as you learn from Step 6 and Step 7 of this book. It's about maintaining a cycle of planning, action, evaluation, and adaptation that keeps you moving toward your dream.

Step 5—Execute Plan—is a pivotal moment in your journey to making your dreams a reality. This is the stage where planning gives way to action, and your dreams begin to take physical shape. A Massive Action Plan isn't just a checklist to be ticked off; it's a commitment to a lifestyle, a different way of thinking, and, most importantly, another way of doing. By taking consistent, focused, and intelligent actions, you bring your goals within reach and prepare yourself for inevitable setbacks and opportunities to pivot and adjust. Remember, execution is where dreams meet reality, and it's through the diligent, consistent application of your action plan that your ambitions will materialize. Let this step be your catalyst, turning your well-laid plans into tangible successes.

Activity for Step 5 - Execute Plan

1. Immediate Kick-off:

Start NOW: Identify one action that you can take immediately toward your goal, no matter how small.

In your composition book, document your starting point, including your status, feelings, and thoughts. This will serve as a reference point for progress.

2. Embrace the 10X Mindset:

Revisit your goals and multiply them by 10. What would it look like? What additional actions would you need to take?

List down areas where you've been holding back or playing it safe, and think of how you can elevate your efforts in these areas tenfold.

3. Create a Weekly Momentum Calendar:

Every Sunday evening or Monday morning, outline your actions for the week. Inspired by ET's "Thank God It's Monday," make Monday your powerhouse day.

Celebrate small successes at the end of each week.

4. Consistency is Key:

Establish daily rituals or habits that directly align with your Massive Action Plan.

Track your daily actions and maintain a streak, challenging yourself to stay consistent.

5. Relentless Action Audit:

At the end of each month, conduct an audit. What actions did you take? What results did they yield? What did you learn?

Adjust your Massive Action Plan based on this monthly audit. Remember, it's a dynamic blueprint.

6. Accountability Partners:

Share your goals and plans with someone who can hold you accountable, preferably from your assembled team.

Schedule regular check-ins with this person or group to review progress, setbacks, and successes.

7. Embrace Setbacks as Stepping-Stones:

When you face a setback, see it as a failure instead of viewing it as feedback.

Document the setback, analyze its cause, adapt, and move forward. Learn from it and improve.

8. Continuous Learning:

Dedicate time to learning new strategies, tools, or skills to help you execute your plan more effectively.

Attend seminars, workshops, or online courses related to your goals.

9. Visualize Success Daily:

Spend a few minutes every day visualizing your end goal. Feel the emotions, picture the success.

This will motivate you and reinforce the urgency and intensity of your actions.

10. Commit to Action, Not Just Results:

While results are crucial, focus on the consistent actions you're taking. Celebrate the effort and the journey.

Understand that results may only sometimes be immediate, but consistent effort will eventually yield success.

11. Create an Action Journal:

Document your daily actions, feelings, challenges, and triumphs.

This journal will serve as a testament to your journey, providing insights and motivation.

12. Pivot When Necessary:

If something isn't working despite consistent efforts, changing the strategy is okay. Remember, the goal remains the same, but the path can change.

The journey toward realizing your dreams is a complex path. It's filled with peaks, valleys, turns, and sometimes U-turns. The power lies not just in the start but in the consistent, relentless actions you take daily, and in your ability to adapt, learn, and persevere. Embrace Step 5 with zeal, knowing that every effort, big or small, takes you closer to your dreams. Let every step be a step of purpose, and soon, you'll find yourself living the dream you once only imagined.

Chapter 14
Step 6 - Fail and Pivot

"Success is stumbling from failure to failure with no loss of enthusiasm." –
~Winston Churchill

Welcome to Step 6: Fail and Pivot. If you're under the impression that the road to success is a straight and smooth, it's time for a reality check. Even the most well-executed plans can and often do fail. But failure isn't the end of the road; it's merely a stepping-stone on the path to success. Take the story of Thomas Edison, for instance. When inventing the light bulb, he famously failed thousands of times. Yet, Edison viewed each failure not as a setback but a lesson, an opportunity to pivot and refine his approach. He once said, "I have not failed. I've just found 10,000 ways that won't work." In this step, you'll learn that failures, setbacks, and roadblocks are inevitable and valuable. Your ability to adapt, pivot, and learn from these moments will play a critical role in how quickly you can turn your dreams into reality.

"I have not failed. I've just found 10,000 ways that won't work."
~Thomas Edison

Many coaches often emphasize that failure is an integral part of the journey to success, but curiously, they rarely include it in their prescribed processes. In contrast, I've deliberately made failure a cornerstone of this plan. Through our missteps, we acquire the insights and knowledge necessary for ultimate success. Recognizing and embracing failure as a valuable teacher allows us to refine our approach and move closer to our objectives.

"Failure is not the opposite of success; it's part of success."
~Arianna Huffington, co-founder of The Huffington Post

Analyzing what went wrong is the first crucial step after experiencing failure. When a particular action or strategy doesn't yield the desired result, evaluating what contributed to that outcome is essential. Was it an issue of poor planning, a lack of resources, or maybe even an external factor that you still needed to consider? Take time to assess your performance metrics, and don't shy away from the uncomfortable details. This deep dive into your failures can be revealing, providing you with the insights you need to make improvements.

Jerry Coy

When people think of modern vacuum cleaners, Dyson often comes to mind. But many don't know that its inventor, Sir James Dyson, faced a challenging journey before achieving success with his innovative vacuum design.

Dyson was frustrated with how traditional vacuum cleaners would lose suction as their bags filled up. This frustration inspired him: he wanted to design a vacuum cleaner that didn't rely on bags and wouldn't lose suction over time. The concept was based on cyclonic separation, a method he observed at a sawmill where it was used to remove sawdust from the air.

Sounds straightforward, right? However, it was far from easy. Dyson created a staggering 5,127 prototypes over five years before he developed a model that he felt was perfect. That's over 5,000 failures and revisions! Each failed prototype brought valuable insights, guiding him closer to his goal.

But the challenges continued. Once he had a working model, no major manufacturer or distributor in the UK wanted to take on his product. They were too invested in the traditional vacuum cleaner models with bags, a significant source of their profit due to replacement sales.

Dyson's pivot came when he decided to manufacture and market the product himself. The first Dyson vacuum cleaner was introduced in Japan, where it was recognized for both its functionality and its unique design. It became a status symbol, and the success there gave Dyson the foothold he needed.

By the late 1990s, the Dyson vacuum cleaner finally entered the UK market and quickly gained a significant share. By 2005, Dyson's dream became a reality as his vacuum design was the market leader in the United States in terms of units sold.

Dyson's journey is a testament to the power of perseverance, the importance of embracing failures as lessons, and the courage to pivot when faced with industry giants who reject innovation.

The next part of dealing with failure is learning from it. This might sound cliche, but it's one of the most overlooked aspects of failure. It's easy to feel discouraged and stop when things don't go as planned, but those who succeed use their failures as learning experiences. Make a list of what you've gained from the experience: whether it's an invaluable lesson, a realization of what not to do, or even just the development of resilience and mental toughness, each failure brings its own set of benefits.

Once you've understood what went wrong and what you can learn from it, it's time to consult your team. A good team is not just there to share in the successes but also invaluable in times of failure. They can provide different perspectives on what went wrong, suggest alternative strategies, and help revise the action plan. Whether it's your mentor pointing out a fundamental flaw in your approach, a colleague offering a different tactic, or even a friend providing emotional support, your team is an essential asset in revising and improving your strategy.

After you've gathered insights from your team, the next step is to revise the plan. Make sure to make necessary adjustments before jumping back in. A plan revision should be based on the collective knowledge gained from the failure and the advice of your team. Update your timelines, set new metrics, and allocate resources differently—do whatever it takes to ensure that your revised plan addresses the weaknesses of the previous one. This newly adjusted plan will be far more robust and better aligned with your goals, giving you a greater chance of success in the next attempt.

"If you don't fail, you're not even trying."
~Denzel Washington

Firstly, one of the most paralyzing forces on the path to achieving your dreams is the fear of failure. This fear can be so overwhelming that it prevents you from taking the first step toward your goals. Before effectively addressing and overcoming this fear, you must acknowledge its existence and understand its roots. Is it a fear of public embarrassment, a fear of wasting time, or perhaps a fear of disappointing yourself or others? The first step in overcoming this debilitating mindset is to recognize that fear is a natural emotional response but should not be allowed to dictate your actions.

Once you've identified the nature of your fear, the next step is to confront it. One practical approach is to reframe how you think about failure. Instead of viewing failure as a devastating end, consider it a valuable lesson in your journey toward success. By shifting your perspective, you make room for constructive experiences, even when things are unplanned. Another strategy is to start small, setting manageable goals that are achievable in the short term. These 'quick wins' can boost your confidence and make the more significant challenge seem more attainable.

Visualization techniques can also be powerful tools to combat fear. Before embarking on a new venture or task, visualize a successful outcome. Create a mental image of success, down to the smallest detail—how it feels, what you're wearing, the environment around you, and even the emotions you'll experience. This vivid mental rehearsal prepares your mind and body for real-world action and can significantly lessen feelings of apprehension.

However, the best way to overcome fear is sometimes to act despite it. The act of 'doing' can often dispel fear and replace it with a sense of accomplishment and empowerment. Starting can be the most challenging part, but momentum is a powerful force. Once you've taken that first step and experienced some level of success or learning, the subsequent steps become easier to tackle. So, arm yourself with a well-thought-out plan, a supportive team, and a positive mindset to conquer your fears and achieve your dreams.

Also, the notion of "failing forward" encourages individuals to embrace setbacks as integral components of their growth journey. Rather than seeing failure as an end or a testament to one's inadequacy, failing forward promotes resilience by positioning every mishap as a lesson learned and a rung on the ladder to success. This mindset is a powerful antidote to the destructive idea that failure is something to be avoided at all costs. By reorienting our perspective on failure, we can take constructive actions post-setback that bring us closer to our ultimate goals.

Jerry Coy

Secondly, societal perspectives often cast failure in a negative light, creating a damaging stigma that hampers individual progress. In many cultures, failure at a task is equated with personal inadequacy, instilling fear and inhibiting potential. By acknowledging and actively combating this societal bias, we can create a more encouraging environment that recognizes failure as an inherent part of the learning and growing process. This way, we free ourselves from needless shame or humiliation and open the path for genuine improvement.

Thirdly, perfectionism, often stemming from societal expectations, can be a significant barrier to growth. While striving for excellence is commendable, an obsession with perfection can be debilitating, fostering a fear of failure that inhibits action. Perfectionism creates an unrealistic standard that, when not met, fuels self-doubt and discourages future efforts. Realizing that perfection is an unattainable ideal can liberate us from the paralysis of fear and empower us to act, flaws and all.

Imposter syndrome is another facet of fear of failure. It's the nagging feeling that you're not as competent as others perceive you to be, accompanied by the fear that you'll be "found out." This syndrome can hinder progress, cause unnecessary stress, and, ironically, make failure more likely by distracting from the task. Practical coping mechanisms like mindfulness exercises, coaching, or even therapy can help manage the emotional weight of this fear. Self-awareness, acceptance, and external support can enable us to overcome imposter syndrome, allowing us to pursue our goals with conviction and confidence.

Deep within the intricate structures of the brain lies the amygdala, a small almond-shaped cluster of nuclei that plays a pivotal role in our emotional responses, especially those related to fear. This ancient part of our brain is responsible for our "fight or flight" response. In prehistoric times, the amygdala helped humans survive by triggering a rapid emotional reaction to potential threats. However, these threats are not often life-threatening predators in the modern world but rather challenges and potential failures. The fear of failure, embarrassment, or judgment can activate the amygdala, urging us to "flee" from the situation or avoid it altogether. This can often manifest as procrastination, avoidance, or settling into our comfort zones where the perceived threats are minimal.

While the comfort zone might seem safe, staying within its boundaries stagnates personal growth and potential for success. Whenever we avoid a challenge or a new experience because of the fear of failure, we reinforce the amygdala's hold on our actions, solidifying our avoidance and inaction patterns. Over time, this can lead to a life of mediocrity and missed opportunities. After all, as the saying goes, "growth and comfort do not coexist." To truly reach our potential, pushing against these boundaries set by our amygdala-driven fears is essential.

One of the most effective ways to override the amygdala's fear response is through gradual exposure. Just as one might overcome a phobia by gradually exposing oneself to the feared object or situation, individuals can desensitize their fear of failure by taking small, calculated risks. The amygdala recognizes these situations as non-threatening by repeatedly facing fears in a controlled environment. Another technique is cognitive reframing. Instead of viewing potential challenges as threats, view them as opportunities for growth and learning.

133

Jerry Coy

Embrace a growth mindset, understanding that failure is not a reflection of one's worth but rather an essential step in the journey of success and personal development. Mindfulness and meditation can also help. By grounding oneself in the present moment, it becomes easier to recognize and understand the amygdala's responses, giving one the clarity to choose a more constructive response. These techniques make it possible to rewire our brain's reaction to fear and step out of our comfort zones, propelling us toward success and fulfillment.

Step 6 emphasizes that failure is not a deterrent but a crucial part of the journey toward success. It challenges traditional perspectives on failure, urging us to "fail forward" by extracting invaluable lessons from each setback. The fear of failure, societal stigma, perfectionism, and even imposter syndrome can all act as barriers, but understanding them is the first step toward overcoming them. By confronting and dismantling these fears, we empower ourselves to take decisive actions and create an environment conducive to growth and development. Therefore, when embarking on your journey toward achieving your dreams, remember that failure is not a pitfall but a stepping-stone, not an end but a new beginning. Don't shy away from it; instead, embrace it, learn from it, and let it propel you closer to your goals.

Chapter 15
Step 7 - Execute Revised Plan

"Our greatest glory is not in never failing, but in rising every time we fail."
– Confucius

I have always admired Sylvester Stallone, not just for his iconic films but more so after learning about his journey. His life's tale is incredibly inspiring. The narrative of his breakout film, "Rocky," which portrays an ordinary man's rise to championship, resonates deeply with his real-life struggles and triumphs. I subscribed to his YouTube channel, "Sly Stallone," for inspiration. I will follow him if he decides to tour as a motivational speaker.

The story of Sylvester Stallone's journey to getting "Rocky" made is a fantastic example of tenacity, belief in oneself, and the willingness to take risks and pivot when necessary.

While this story has been recounted in numerous interviews and articles over the years, one of the primary sources where Stallone discussed his early struggles and the "Rocky" journey is the documentary

"Sylvester Stallone: An Original," which provides a detailed look into his life and career.

Sylvester Stallone was no stranger to adversity. Before becoming an icon in the film industry, he faced countless rejections and struggled financially. Stallone had a dream and a screenplay for "Rocky," but selling it was no easy task.

In the mid-1970s, Stallone was an unknown actor with a dream. He wrote the screenplay for "Rocky" in three days, drawing from his experiences and observations of the boxing world. When he tried to sell the script, he encountered numerous rejections. Film studios hesitated to take a risk on an unknown actor with a screenplay centered on an underdog.

Things got so tough that Stallone desperately sold his beloved dog Butkus for $50 (the exact amount is often debated) to help pay his bills. It was a heartbreaking decision that he felt was necessary at the time.

Finally, a studio expressed interest in his screenplay, offering him a substantial amount. However, there was a catch: they didn't want him to star in it. Despite his financial struggles, Stallone believed in his vision for "Rocky" and wanted to play the lead role. He turned down the offer, a risky move considering his circumstances.

His persistence paid off. The studio eventually agreed to let him star in the movie, although for a much smaller payment for the script. The resulting film, "Rocky," became a massive hit, winning three Oscars, including Best Picture, and turning Stallone into a star overnight.

Later, with the money he earned from the film, Stallone tracked down the man he sold his dog to and repurchased it, reuniting with his loyal companion. To convince the man to sell back the dog, Stallone offered him a small part in "Rocky" to entice him to sell it back at a substantially higher amount. You can see that guy and Butkus in "Rocky."

Stallone's story, much like Rocky Balboa's, is one of perseverance, resilience, and believing in oneself even when faced with insurmountable odds. It's a testament to the power of passion and the importance of staying true to one's vision.

In Step 7, we arrive at a critical juncture—executing the revised plan. This is more than a mere repetition of Step 5; it's a nuanced, recalibrated approach born from the insights and lessons gleaned from our failures in Step 6. Failure has taught us what doesn't work, so we are better equipped to refine our strategies. It's a moment to rekindle our motivation, reevaluate, and perhaps even adjust our goals and sub-goals. Importantly, any adjustments should still align with our overarching dreams, the essence of why we embarked on this journey. So, this isn't just about doing the same things better; it's about doing better things, more imaginative execution, and a renewed commitment to our vision. This is the step where we use our newfound wisdom and experience as fuel to propel us closer to the life we aspire to lead.

In revising your action plan, it's crucial not to overlook your team—the invaluable people you've enlisted to help manifest your vision. Step 7 also involves aligning your team with the new course of action. A transparent update on what went wrong, what you've learned, and how you plan to correct the course is essential. This open line of communication keeps everyone on the same page and fosters a sense of collective ownership and responsibility. Furthermore, your team's motivation is just as important as your own. Inspire them with renewed vigor, reignite their commitment to the mission, and ensure they share the excitement and optimism that come with this fresh start. After all, a motivated team is productive, and their enthusiasm can significantly influence the success of your revised plan.

Staying ambitious is vital, especially when you're executing a revised plan. Challenges and setbacks can be disheartening, but it's essential to maintain the ambition that initially fueled your journey. Keep your eyes on the target; let your long-term goals guide you as you adjust. Even though you're revising your approach, your ultimate dream should remain the same. This will serve as your North Star, helping you navigate the complexities and uncertainties that inevitably arise. Revising your plan should mean something other than scaling back your ambitions but fine-tuning your path to achieving them. The hurdles you've faced should strengthen your resolve, not weaken it. Keep the big picture in view and let it renew your determination to reach your lofty objectives.

Revisiting your written goals and dreams displayed on your vision board can be an incredibly effective motivator, especially when executing a revised plan. Seeing your aspirations in writing or through images can rekindle the original passion and enthusiasm that led you to set those goals in the first place. When you hit a stumbling block or experience a setback, return to that vision board and remind yourself why you started this journey. Let the vision board act as your anchor, steadying you when the seas of life get rough.

In addition to your vision board, maintaining an "accountability mirror" can further engrain your commitments into your daily life.

Write your revised goals and key action steps on sticky notes or directly on the mirror you investigate daily. This daily visual reinforcement keeps your objectives fresh, fortifying your resolve to meet them. It's like having a daily meeting with yourself, a constant reminder of what you have promised to achieve and who you aspire to become.

These tangible practices can help keep you on track, but remember they are most effective when used in concert. Your vision board encapsulates your long-term dreams, while your accountability mirror breaks those dreams down into manageable, daily actions. As you adjust and encounter new challenges, keep both updated. They're not static representations but living, evolving guides that should change as you grow and learn. By consistently reverting to these physical reminders, you can stay aligned with your ambitious goals and keep pushing forward, no matter your obstacles.

Stepping out of your comfort zone is essential for personal and professional growth. When you stick to what's comfortable, you tell yourself and the world that you are content with your current state. But the transformative power of personal evolution lies in the unfamiliar and the challenging. Your comfort zone is a behavioral space where your activities and behaviors fit a routine and pattern that minimizes stress and risk. While this provides emotional security, it also creates boundaries beyond which lie all your untapped potential.

Taking risks, trying new things, and putting yourself in unfamiliar situations can yield substantial personal growth and make achieving your goals an exciting and fulfilling journey. The initial discomfort you feel when stepping outside your familiar bounds often gives way to more excellent skills, expanded knowledge, and increased self-confidence. The accomplishment of something that initially scared you is intoxicating and can motivate you to tackle even more significant challenges.

Remember, your dreams and goals often reside on the other side of what you're comfortable doing. By regularly challenging yourself to go beyond the familiar, you're also teaching yourself to become more adaptable, a crucial skill in our ever-changing world. Take baby steps or leaps—consistently move away from what's comfortable and toward what will make you grow. This is how you'll move closer to your ultimate dreams and ambitions.

After encountering a setback, the first action is acknowledging your failure. It's essential to look at it as neither a downfall nor a dead-end but rather a stepping-stone on your journey. Far from being fatal, a failure is a priceless lesson that brings you closer to your ultimate objective. This cognitive shift from viewing failure as a negative to understanding it as a learning experience is critical.

Once you've acknowledged and learned from your failure, the next step is cultivating resilience. This emotional resilience becomes your psychological shield against future setbacks. With a resilient mindset, you're not easily discouraged; instead, you're prepared to face the challenges that will inevitably come your way. You'll find that each challenge becomes less daunting and your reaction to it more effective.

Another crucial aspect of executing a revised plan is flexibility and adaptability. The world continually changes, and a rigid plan will soon become outdated. Be ready to pivot your strategy and make real-time adjustments. Think of your plan as a living document that evolves to meet new circumstances and capitalize on fresh opportunities.

Never underestimate the importance of celebrating small victories along the way. These wins, however minor they may seem, serve as motivation boosters. They validate your time and effort and renew your energy for future challenges. Acknowledging your progress can be incredibly empowering and keep you on the path toward your larger goals.

Rather than waiting for another failure to reassess and adjust your approach, make continuous refinement a part of your routine. Keep a close eye on the metrics that matter to you and align your daily actions with your overarching objectives. Constant adjustments keep you in sync with your goals and make your journey more efficient and effective.

Lastly, when the going gets tough—especially following a setback—return to your 'why.' Revisiting the core reasons behind your dreams and goals can reignite your passion and focus. Your motivation and how become clearer when you deeply understand why you're pursuing something. Remember 'why' you started in the first place.

You may reencounter failure as you strive to make your dreams come true. And that's okay. Remember, failure is not a dead end but a detour on the road to success. If you find yourself facing setbacks once more, don't get disheartened. Instead, go back to Step 6, analyze what went wrong, revise your plan with your team, and learn valuable lessons from the experience. Then, proceed to Step 7, executing your updated action plan with renewed focus and motivation. The journey toward achieving your dreams is rarely a straight path; it's like a labyrinth full of twists and turns. Each time you loop back to Steps 6 and 7, you're not starting over; you're leveraging your accumulated wisdom to move forward more effectively. Keep iterating through this process until your dreams are fully realized. Remember, it's not about how many times you fall but how many times you get up and keep moving.

"Each time you loop back from Pivot to Fail, you're not starting over. You're leveraging your accumulated wisdom to move forward more effectively." ~Jerry Coy

---

Step 7 is about taking thoughtful action, armed with the wisdom and lessons learned from your previous failures. It's not merely a repetition of Step 5; it's an evolved, more strategic version of your action plan. It's an opportunity to align your team with your renewed focus, adjust your goals for maximum impact, and reinvigorate your drive. As you move forward, continually revisit your written goals and vision board to keep your eye on the prize, and don't shy away from discomfort—stepping out of your comfort zone is where growth happens. Most importantly, remember that setbacks are just setups for comebacks. Each revision of your plan takes you one step closer to manifesting your dreams into reality.

Chapter 16
Bonus Step 8 – Transcendence

"What a man can be, he must be.
This need we call self-actualization."
~Abraham Maslow

Abraham Maslow initially proposed his hierarchy of needs in 1943 in his paper "A Theory of Human Motivation," published in the journal "Psychological Review." However, it was only later in life that he discussed the idea of "transcendence" as an extension of self-actualization. This concept was articulated in his later writings, such as the posthumously published book "The Farther Reaches of Human Nature" (1971).

The following quote encapsulates the experience of those who've reached a level of self-actualization and transcendence where they can continually find joy and wonder in the simple, fundamental aspects of life.

"The most fortunate are those who have a wonderful capacity to appreciate again and again, freshly and naively, the basic goods of life, with awe, pleasure, wonder, and even ecstasy."
~Abraham Maslow

In this work, Maslow proposes that beyond self-actualization lies the realm of transcendence, where individuals achieve their fullest potential and seek to help others reach the same heights. The idea of transcendence suggests that the journey of self-fulfillment extends into the well-being of others, connecting one's self-actualization to the greater good.

The journey to achieving your dreams continues even after you've executed your revised plan (Step 7) and achieved your dream. Much like Abraham Maslow's later addition of "Transcendence" to his hierarchy of needs, there's a step beyond self-actualization that often involves helping others reach their potential. Maslow's concept of transcendence involves not just achieving your own goals and fulfilling your potential but also facilitating and enabling the growth, development, and actualization of others. Adding a "Bonus Step 8: Transcendence" to the "Start on Your Dreams" framework captures this notion eloquently.

After successfully navigating the initial seven steps, your experiences—triumphs and setbacks—become a treasure trove of wisdom and guidance for the next generation. You have a unique perspective that can serve as both a roadmap and a source of inspiration for others. This aligns with Maslow's belief that the ultimate form of self-actualization is transcending one's needs and aspirations to assist others in their quests. Whether by mentoring, teaching or simply sharing your journey openly, you become a guiding light for those at earlier stages of their path.

The act of helping others reach their dreams can be gratifying. Not only does it provide a sense of fulfillment and purpose, but it also adds a layer of meaning to your achievements. Your dreams don't exist in isolation; they become part of a larger narrative, a collective aspiration toward growth, development, and enrichment. The satisfaction derived from seeing others achieve their goals, knowing you played a part in their journey, can be incredibly gratifying.

In a practical sense, helping others also offers the opportunity for self-reflection and further growth. Teaching and mentoring require you to articulate your experiences and the lessons you've learned, deepening your understanding and even revealing insights you may not have fully appreciated. This continual process of learning and self-discovery further enriches your life, offering a path for ongoing personal development even after you've achieved your initial dreams.

So, as a "Bonus Step 8," Transcendence aligns seamlessly with the foundational principles laid out in this book. It serves as both an extension and a culmination of your journey. By giving back to the next generation, you enrich their lives and perpetuate a cycle of growth, inspiration, and collective betterment that makes the entire process even more meaningful and fulfilling.

In Step 8—Transcendence, we explore a facet of success beyond the self: the commitment to elevating others. Reaching your dreams is a monumental achievement, but the real magic happens when you turn around to lend a hand to those coming up behind you. This concept echoes Maslow's notion of self-transcendence, emphasizing not just personal growth but the growth of others. As someone who has walked this path and tasted success, my role as a teacher and the reason I've written this book and created a podcast is to share what I've learned to help you reach your summit.

The circle of achievement shouldn't stop with you. Become that beacon for others as you've gleaned wisdom and strategies from those who've walked before you. You create a ripple effect that could span generations by sharing your experiences, tools, and lessons. This is a legacy far more enduring than any singular achievement.

My journey in teaching, writing, and podcasting is not just a personal endeavor but a way to fulfill this final step of Transcendence. I want to offer you a set of tactics for success and a sustainable model that you can share. So, as you revel in your accomplishments, remember that ultimate fulfillment comes from elevating others. Whether you mentor, share wisdom through a book, launch a podcast, or guide someone with authentic conversations, know that your influence can shape not just one life but potentially millions.

In this spirit of Transcendence, you're not just chasing dreams but also fueling the dreams of others. You transition from being merely successful to being significant. And that, in the grand tapestry of life, is a success story that truly stands the test of time.

Chapter 17
Assessments and Reflections

In our fast-paced world, we often find ourselves racing toward our goals, seldom pausing to catch our breath or look around. But imagine navigating a vast ocean without occasionally checking the stars or embarking on a cross-country journey without glancing at a map. The chance of losing our way increases exponentially. Such is the journey toward our dreams without the guideposts of assessment and reflection.

Assessment and reflection are not mere bureaucratic exercises or checkpoints. They are profound, deeply personal endeavors that have the power to shape the trajectory of our aspirations. They offer us a mirror, a lens through which we can view our actions, decisions, and the paths we tread. We gain clarity about our progress through assessments, ensuring we remain aligned with our objectives. Reflection, on the other hand, delves deeper. It is a soulful exploration of our experiences, emotions, and the lessons learned along the way.

This chapter uncovers the symbiotic relationship between assessments and reflections in our journey of self-growth and dream realization. It offers a compass and a beacon—tools to ensure we do so with purpose, understanding, and authenticity as we move forward.

Power of Assessment

Assessments illuminate beacons in the vast landscape of personal and professional development, casting light on our strengths, weaknesses, and the intricate dynamics that define our personality and behavior. These structured evaluations, while rooted in logic and methodology, offer insights that can be profoundly transformative.

Picture this: as an individual navigating through life's many challenges, one often finds oneself standing at a crossroads, pondering the right path to take. Here, assessments act as guides, helping decode the complex maze of our psyche. By offering a structured analysis of our skills, attitudes, and potential, they provide clear signposts for growth and improvement.

However, assessments are not just cold, analytical tools; they can be deeply personal. When you delve into the results of a comprehensive assessment, it's akin to holding up a mirror to your soul. While sometimes surprising, the revelations are a testament to the intricate complexities that make up human nature. Embracing these findings allows for a richer understanding of oneself, facilitating a journey of introspection and growth.

In the professional realm, assessments play a pivotal role. Imagine a corporate environment where individuals, teams, and leaders continually strive for excellence. Here, assessments serve a dual purpose.

On the one hand, they aid in identifying potential leaders, individuals whose skills and temperaments make them prime candidates for future responsibilities. On the other hand, they also pinpoint areas of improvement, ensuring that training and resources are channeled effectively.

However, assessments go beyond just individual introspection and corporate evaluations. In educational settings, they mold the path of young minds, highlighting strengths and areas of interest and guiding students toward fields where their passions and talents align. This early intervention can shape careers, ensuring a future where work aligns with passion and aptitude.

In essence, the power of assessment is its ability to provide clarity in a world brimming with uncertainties. By offering tangible, actionable insights, estimates become the bedrock on which personal and professional journeys are built, ensuring that every step taken is one towards growth, understanding, and excellence.

In the rush of today's fast-paced world, reflection stands as an oasis of introspection and self-understanding. Unlike the black-and-white evaluations that assessments offer, reflection delves deeper, providing a rich tapestry of our experiences, thoughts, feelings, and the intricate interplay between them. This seemingly simple introspection is the cornerstone of actual personal growth.

One of the most profound outcomes of reflection is the journey to self-awareness. Through the quiet contemplation of our actions, decisions, and experiences, we slowly peel back the layers of our psyche. This process reveals our deepest beliefs, values, and motivations, shining light on the forces that propel or hold us back. The beauty of this self-awareness is its ability to illuminate not just our past behaviors but also to shape our future ones.

As we move through life, we are constantly bombarded with experiences that evoke a spectrum of emotions. From the dizzying highs of success to the soul-crushing lows of failure, our emotional palette continually expands and evolves. Reflection is a therapeutic tool, allowing us to process and integrate these emotions. It converts raw, often overwhelming emotions into powerful lessons, providing closure and clarity.

Furthermore, our goals and aspirations can often become muddled amidst the noise and chaos of daily life. Reflection acts as the compass, constantly recalibrating our journey and ensuring we remain true to our core desires and objectives. Setting aside moments for introspection allows us to sift through external distractions and internal conflicts, bringing our genuine aspirations back into sharp focus.

It's also worth noting the incredible relationship between reflection and creativity. Far removed from the structured world of assessments and evaluations, reflecting stimulates the mind, allowing it to roam freely. This unbridled exploration often leads to innovative ideas and fresh perspectives. Many of history's greatest thinkers attribute their breakthroughs to moments of quiet contemplation.

Moreover, reflection is the anvil upon which resilience and emotional intelligence are forged. By repeatedly confronting and understanding our vulnerabilities, fears, and insecurities, we become more robust and better equipped to navigate life's challenges. This emotional maturity enhances our interactions with others and deepens our relationship with ourselves.

The art of reflection is about more than just understanding the past. It's a dynamic tool that gives us insights and understanding, empowering us to sculpt a future filled with purpose, clarity, and wisdom.

In the journey of self-awareness and growth, various paths lead to the same destination of introspection and understanding. One of the timeless avenues is journaling. Imagine sitting in a quiet corner, pen poised over paper, ready to pour out the day's experiences, thoughts, and emotions. This simple act offers a unique catharsis, allowing one to decode complex emotions and see patterns emerge over time.

Yet, for those who find the vast canvas of an empty page daunting, guided reflection provides direction. It's akin to having a wise friend ask, "What challenged you today?" or "How did that experience shape your understanding?" Such prompts can act as beacons, guiding the wandering mind toward the shores of clarity.

Then, there's the ancient art of meditation and mindfulness. Beyond its spiritual connotations, it serves as a tool for reflection. Picture a tranquil setting where one sits, eyes closed, focusing on the present moment, connecting deeply with every experience and emotion. This mindful practice peels away layers of superficiality, revealing insights that often remain hidden in the chaos of daily life.

However, reflection is only sometimes a solitary endeavor. Peer reflection offers a window to view oneself from another's perspective.

Engaging in heartfelt conversations with a trusted friend or mentor can mirror one's experiences, bringing forth insights that might have been overlooked in isolation.

Visual thinkers often find solace in visual reflection. It's like crafting a tapestry of one's thoughts, emotions, and experiences. Through mind maps or vision boards, one can weave intricate patterns that depict one's inner world, providing a tangible representation of one's reflections.

Setting a rhythm in reflection is crucial, and time-based reflection ensures this consistency. Whether it's the tranquil moments of dawn or a dedicated weekend every month, these periodic introspections act as milestones in one's reflective journey.

In this era, technology is present. Tech-assisted reflection harnesses the power of the digital age, with apps that prompt journal entries or mood trackers that chart emotional landscapes over time, acting as modern companions in this age-old practice.

Lastly, the call of the wild, where nature immersion beckons. The rustling leaves, chirping birds, and the gentle flow of a stream offer the perfect symphony for reflection. Away from the hustle, surrounded by nature, one finds a space that magnifies inner voices, facilitating deep introspection.

In the grand tapestry of life, these techniques serve as threads, each unique yet intertwined, leading one towards a richer understanding of oneself and the world around.

Jerry Coy

Incorporating Assessments and Reflections in the 7-Step System

The journey of realizing dreams is dynamic. It's filled with highs, lows, crossroads, and detours. Just as a sailor uses a compass and stars to navigate the vast oceans, the 7-Step System can significantly benefit from incorporating assessments and reflections.

As you embark on the first step, Define Your Dreams, it's essential to assess the origin of these dreams. Are they indeed yours, or have external factors influenced them? Reflection can provide clarity, ensuring that the dreams you chase genuinely resonate with your innermost desires.

Reflective practices can be instrumental when you progress to Setting Your Goals in Step 2. There needs to be more than just setting goals; one must understand the 'why' behind them. This deeper understanding is gleaned through introspection, ensuring your goals align with your core values and long-term visions.

Creating a Massive Action Plan in Step 3 involves strategizing and planning. Periodic assessments are crucial here. They help determine if the path you've charted is the most efficient or if tweaks are necessary. Regular reflection can bring to light new insights or methods you hadn't considered initially.

As you Assemble Your Team in Step 4, assessments play a pivotal role in gauging the strengths and weaknesses of team members. Simultaneously, reflecting on team dynamics can lead to a more harmonious and synergistic relationship among members, ensuring everyone pulls in the same direction.

Step 5 emphasizes the importance of Executing the Plan. Here, consistent assessments are crucial to monitor progress. Conversely, reflection ensures that you remain grounded, learning from each phase of execution and making informed decisions as you move forward.

When you encounter setbacks and need to Fail and Pivot in Step 6, assessments provide the data necessary to understand where things went awry. Reflections, during this phase, become deeply personal. They guide you in finding resilience, understanding the lessons hidden in failures, and gathering the strength to pivot effectively.

Lastly, as you Execute the Revised Plan in Step 7, assessments ensure that the changes made are effective. At this juncture, reflections help balance persistence and flexibility, ensuring you remain adaptable yet focused on your end goal.

Incorporating assessments and reflections into the 7-Step System is like adding a compass and a map to a traveler's backpack. While the journey is uniquely yours, these tools ensure that you remain oriented, make informed decisions, and, most importantly, stay true to your essence. As you traverse this path towards your dreams, let regular assessments be your checkpoints and reflections be your guiding stars, leading you towards success with a deep sense of fulfillment.

Jerry Coy

Chapter 18
Summary and Conclusion

"What lies behind and before us are tiny matters compared to what lies within us."
~Ralph Waldo Emerson

In the journey to achieve our dreams, we've navigated seven crucial steps, each designed to propel us closer to our ultimate goals. We began by purging negativity and clearing the mental space for constructive thinking. Then, we focused on infusing positivity and altering our mindset to eradicate blame and cultivate responsibility. Step 3 called for adopting routines and habits, building the scaffolding upon which our dreams could take shape.

We further sharpened our focus with Step 4, putting the right team in place to facilitate the journey. Here, we learned that success is rarely a solo venture; it often involves a harmonious collective of dedicated individuals. Step 5 ushered in action, cutting through procrastination and hesitation with decisive measures to enact our plans. Yet, plans often face obstacles; Step 6 addressed this by embracing failure

156

and pivoting as fundamental elements of the process, teaching us to learn and adapt.

Step 7 had us execute revised plans, incorporating newfound wisdom from our setbacks. We revisited our teams, reassessed our goals, and renewed our dedication to the mission. This led us to the bonus Step 8—Transcendence—where the focus shifted from personal success to elevating others, from being merely successful to genuinely significant.

In essence, these steps create a cycle rather than a linear path. Even after achieving one dream, new aspirations will surface. It's a never-ending journey of growth, setbacks, learnings, and, most importantly, elevating others. So, as you stand on the threshold of your dreams, remember that each step has prepared you for this moment, and the journey ahead is just another chapter waiting to be written. May you embrace each phase with the passion and resilience it deserves, and may your dreams and those you inspire take flight.

Achieving one's dreams is not a mere chance but a result of conscious decisions, careful planning, and dedicated execution. Our journey together through this book has been rooted in a 7-step system designed to provide clarity, structure, and a path to transform your dreams into tangible realities.

1. Define Your Dreams: Recognizing and defining your dreams is the first and perhaps most critical step. Every incredible journey begins with a vision, and your dreams provide that beacon of hope, guiding you toward your desired destination.

Jerry Coy

2. Set Your Goals: Dreams provide direction, but goals are the milestones you'll use to measure progress. They're specific, measurable, achievable, relevant, and time-bound aspects that structure the otherwise abstract notion of dreams.

3. Massive Action Plan: Without action, dreams remain intangible. Designing a robust action plan ensures that every step moves you closer to your goal, big or small.

4. Assemble Your Team: No one achieves greatness in isolation. Surrounding oneself with a supportive team and mentors speeds up the process. These individuals provide guidance, motivation, and expertise, helping navigate the hurdles.

5. Execute Plan: Taking systematic and consistent action is pivotal. It's about commitment, consistency, and moving forward even when the going gets tough.

6. Fail and Pivot: Failure isn't the end; in many ways, it's a beginning. It's a learning opportunity, offering insights that help recalibrate and adjust the strategy to align better with the desired outcome.

7. Execute Revised Plan: Armed with the lessons from previous missteps, it's crucial to approach the task with renewed vigor and a refined plan. Significant and minor adjustments can make a world of difference in outcomes.

Our journey together also touched upon essential life principles such as the significance of meditation, the power of mindfulness, and the profound impact of good habits. We delved into the importance of nurturing the right friendships, the role of mentors, and the continual reminder that our environment often shapes our outcomes.

It's also worth noting the guidance drawn from various thought leaders, from Stephen Covey's profound habits to Tony Robbins' insights, Grant Cardone's audacious strategies, and Arianna Huffington's balanced approach to life. Every insight serves as a tool in your arsenal, ensuring you're well-equipped to face every challenge that comes your way.

Dreams are not just the figments of our imagination; they are the very essence of what makes life worth living. The journey to achieving them may be riddled with challenges, but everything is attainable with the right strategy, support, and mindset. The 7-step system and the wisdom drawn from various experts are your roadmap. As you close this book, remember: Your dreams await and are worth every effort. So, set forth with conviction, passion, and the unyielding belief that you can and will make them come true.

Jerry Coy

Chapter 19
Examples

Example 1: I want six-pack abs.

Step 1: Define Your Dreams

Start by clearly stating what your dream looks like. In this case, the dream is to have a fit, healthy body with visible six-pack abs. Visualize how you will look and feel when you achieve this dream. Ask yourself, "Why do I want six-pack abs?"

Step 2: Set Your Goals

Break down the dream into specific, measurable, and time-bound goals. For example, "Achieve 10% body fat and visibly defined six-pack abs in 6 months."

Step 3: Massive Action Plan

Outline a comprehensive action plan to achieve your goals. This could involve a combination of a diet plan, a workout routine focusing on core strength, and regular body measurement sessions. Include daily, weekly, and monthly tasks to keep you on track.

Step 4: Assemble Your Team

Gather the people who can guide you and help you execute your plan. This could be a fitness trainer for your workouts, a nutritionist for diet advice, and perhaps friends or family members to serve as accountability partners.

Step 5: Execute Plan

With your plan and team in place, it's time to take immediate action. Start your workout routine and diet plan immediately. No "I'll start on Monday" or "New Year, New Me"—do it now.

Step 6: Fail and Pivot

If, for some reason, you don't see the results you expected, keep going. This is a chance to learn and adjust. Speak to your team about what went wrong and make necessary adjustments to your Massive Action Plan.

Step 7: Execute Revised Plan

With the adjustments made, launch back into execution mode. You may need to revise your goals or timeline, but that's okay. Keep your eyes on your dream, and don't let short-term setbacks discourage you.

Example 2: I want to own a coffee shop.

Step 1: Define Your Dreams

First, articulate your dream in as much detail as possible. Instead of saying, "I want to own a coffee shop," describe what kind of coffee shop you want. Maybe you envision a community-focused café with locally sourced beans and a cozy atmosphere for artists and students to hang out. Write this vision down and keep it somewhere visible, like on a vision board.

Step 2: Set Your Goals

Next, set specific, measurable, ambitious, and time-bound goals to bring you closer to your dream. One goal could be to "Secure financing for the coffee shop within six months." Another could be "Find a suitable location in X neighborhood within three months."

Step 3: Massive Action Plan

Create a comprehensive action plan outlining the steps needed to achieve each goal. This could include researching how to start a business, speaking with bank representatives about loans, and finding mentors in the coffee shop industry.

Step 4: Assemble Your Team

Your dream of owning a coffee shop is something you should tackle with others. Bring together a team to help you succeed, such as a business advisor, real estate agent, and even baristas with experience. Keep this team motivated and aligned with your vision.

Step 5: Execute Plan

Start executing your Massive Action Plan. Take concrete steps every day that move you closer to your goals. Be consistent and stay committed.

Step 6: Fail and Pivot

Failure is not only likely but also an essential part of the journey. If a location falls through or your financing doesn't come in as planned, keep going. Learn from these setbacks, consult your team for additional insights, and adjust your plan as needed.

Step 7: Execute Revised Plan

Now that you've gained more information and refined your strategy, execute your revised plan. Continue to consult your written goals and your team, and keep an eye on your timeline to stay focused and on track.

Jerry Coy

References (Suggested Reading)

Myga, K.A., Kuehn, E. & Azanon, E. (2022). Autosuggestion: A cognitive process that empowers your brain. *Experimental Brain Research,* *240*(3), 381–394. (https://doi.org/10.1007/s00221-021-06265-8)

Mandolesi, L. et al. (2018). Effects of Physical Exercise on Cognitive Functioning and Wellbeing: Biological and Psychological Benefits. *Frontiers in Psychology, 9(*509). (doi:10.3389/fpsyg.2018.00509)

Covey, S.R. *7 Habits of Highly Effective People* (www.quickmba.com)

Matthews, G. (2007). The Impact of Commitment, Accountability, and Written Goals on Goal Achievement. *Psychology | Faculty Presentations* (https://scholar.dominican.edu/psychology-faculty-conference-presentations/3)

Goggins, D. *Can't Hurt Me: Master Your Mind and Defy the Odds.*

Cardone, G. *The 10X Rule: The Only Difference Between Success and Failure.*

Hill, N. *Think and Grow Rich*

Robbins, T. *Awaken the Giant Within.*

Huffington, A. *Thrive: The Third Metric to Redefining Success and Creating a Life of Well-Being, Wisdom, and Wonder.*

Maslow, A.H. (1971). *The Farther Reaches of Human Nature.* Viking Press.

Clear, J. *Atomic Habits: An Easy & Proven Way to Build Good Habits & Break Bad Ones.*

Newport, C. (2012). *So Good They Can't Ignore You: Why Skills Trump Passion in the Quest for Work You Love.* Grand Central Publishing.

Hardy, D. *The Compound Effect: Jumpstart Your Income, Your Life, Your Success.* Da Capo Lifelong Books, 2010.

Tolle, E. (1997). *The Power of Now: A Guide to Spiritual Enlightenment.* New World Library.

For more suggested reading, visit: *startonyourdreams.com/reading*

Be on the lookout for the companion journal workbook, my next creation.

About The Author

Jerry Coy is a Navy veteran who honorably served aboard a submarine and is a lifelong learner with a diverse professional background. After acquiring a BS degree in Kinesiology from Arizona State University, he embarked on an 18-year journey in physiotherapy as an LMT. However, his inherent passion for molding young minds led him to transition into the realm of education, where he now thrives as a science teacher.

Family has always been the cornerstone of Jerry's life; he's a dedicated husband and a proud father to three adopted daughters and one son. During the challenging times of the COVID-19 pandemic, Jerry's commitment to his students shone brightly. During these trying times, he developed the 7-step system, a strategic approach initially designed to motivate his students. Since then, he has continually refined this method, ensuring it serves as a beacon for all those navigating their personal and professional aspirations. Through this book, Jerry combines his vast experience with his profound dedication to empowerment, exemplifying his unwavering commitment to guiding others toward their dreams.

www.ingramcontent.com/pod-product-compliance
Lightning Source LLC
Chambersburg PA
CBHW030257130626
46549CB00002B/580